T0197105

THE OBJECT PARADE

THE OBJECT PARADE

THE OBJECT PARADE

DINAH LENNEY

COUNTERPOINT
BERKELEY

Copyright © 2014 by Dinah Lenney

All rights reserved under International and Pan-American Copyright Conventions. No part of this book may be used or reproduced in any manner whatsoever without written permission from the publisher, except in the case of brief quotations embodied in critical articles and reviews.

Library of Congress Cataloging-in-Publication Data
Lenney, Dinah.
The object parade : essays / Dinah Lenney.
pages cm
ISBN 978-1-61902-300-0 (hardback)
1. Lenney, Dinah. 2. Actresses—United States—Biography. I. Title.
PN2287.L425A3 2014
791.4302—8092—dc23
[B]
2013044917

Paperback ISBN: 978-1-61902-539-4

Interior design by Sabrina Plomitallo-González, Neuwirth & Associates

COUNTERPOINT
2560 Ninth Street, Suite 318
Berkeley, CA 94710
www.counterpointpress.com

Printed in the United States of America

for Fred

I am giving you this because I love you. Or because it was given to me. Because I bought it somewhere special. Because you will care for it. Because it will complicate your life.

—Edmund de Waal, *The Hare with the Amber Eyes*

The object . . . has no duty whatsoever toward me, it is I who am obliged to it.   —Francis Ponge, *Mute Objects of Affection*

PROLOGUE

IN THE BEGINNING — or somewhere in the middle actually—there was a parade. A parade of objects. Around a schoolyard. On a weekday morning, bright but unseasonably cold. At the appointed hour everybody—children, teachers, parents, staff—spilled out of classrooms and offices and cars, and congregated on one side of the blacktop. On the other, the calvacade assembled. My son Jake, nine or ten at the time, got in line with his mates, head, arms, and legs sticking out of a box, turquoise, equipped with a long antenna (also turquoise) and a speaker/receiver, a slightly sloping grid of black dots, painted on its face.

It had rained the night before. I remember iridescent puddles on the two-ball courts. How they mirrored pieces of clouds, along with wiggling oblongs of red, green, gold, purple, (turquoise), poster paint colors; how the objects, shivering in anticipation and because of the chill, squeezed themselves into wedges of sunshine here and there. And then it began, to scattered cheers and applause, the kids hushed and shuffling at first, solemn and shy, but, as they rounded the first corner, increasingly jubilant: first, the isolated hop or skip, then, as if a spring had been released or a switch flicked, an exuberance of jumping and running and whooping and shouting. The occasional shove, too, of course; the elbow stuck, the heel caught, the stumble and cry, when they'd halt as one, for the pencil, who'd lost his eraser, rescued before it rolled into the wet, or the turquoise walkie-talkie who'd stopped to right his antenna, which, from the beginning, tacked to one side.

Why aren't there pictures? There ought to be pictures. What I wouldn't give for an image or two, alongside this hubbub of recall, of various stages of planning and building and stepping around kids on the linoleum, or looking over the tops of their heads where they sat at low tables, all of them absorbed in some phase of creation—drawing, mixing (newspaper and paste), molding, painting.

I remember that pencil, number two, mustard yellow, four feet tall; and assorted fruits and vegetables; a violin, a candlestick, a spoon, a fork, a baseball bat. Was there a box of cereal? Yes—yes, I can see it, Fruit Loops, I think it was, or possibly Captain Crunch—it came up to my shoulders. And I know there was a bottle of nail polish, waist-high. Also a globe, slightly misshapen. A football. A bowling pin, a teddy bear, an alarm clock. Some forty objects, there being forty kids, third and fourth graders, in all. And the reason for the event? Celebration, culmination—a curricular punctuation point—having to do with the theory that children will *understand* the world if they build it for themselves. Therefore each child had picked something, some *thing*: taken it apart for science and math, researched its history and cultural relevance for social studies, described it in prose and poetry for language arts, and then sculpted it from papier mache, pungent at first, and then crusty and ubiquitous (for weeks it came home in their hair and their laces and under their nails), to wear in the Object Parade.

But how did they choose? For themselves for the most part, in spite of opinionated parents and siblings—from the strange, the familiar, the real, the imagined, the old, the new; from animal, vegetable, mineral, edible. It was Jake's idea to be a walkie talkie, and he wanted to be blue—at which point we did wield our influence; convinced him that turquoise was *almost* blue (he pretended to be convinced anyway) since otherwise he'd have marched as a navy blue blob, no distinguishing features. But as determined as I was to change his mind, I didn't ask why—why blue? Why that shade?—just assumed it was because dark blue was his favorite. Later, long afterwards, I realized: Jake had been given walkie talkies as a present a year or two before. And think of the adventures—consider the possibilities (this before cell phones)—the thrill of whispering from upstairs to down, from out back to out front, as if from the earth to the moon, from Alaska to the Amazon, from New York to L.A. Eventually, as happens, one of the pair got wet, or crushed, or lost, or was only misplaced, by which time the novelty had mostly worn off: still, blue-black they were, the originals, and they'd enjoyed unprecedented status and play. I should have understood, aesthetic considerations aside—it was the truth Jake was after for the Object Parade; the deep and resonating satisfaction and reward of memory faithfully and authentically revealed.

But is that why he wasn't especially attached to the replica-in-turquoise? Because cooperative as he'd been about the color, it was just all wrong? I wonder—I even wondered at the time why he didn't seem to notice, much less protest, when I took the big-as-life walkie talkie down to the basement, where it nonetheless continued to get in the way. Every time I pulled out a suitcase or went looking for last year's tax return it toppled in my path until one day I finally dragged it out the back door, up the side of the house and onto the street, along with a hockey stick, a pair of crutches, and an old computer console. There it sat in the gutter with the rest, chipped and misshapen, its antenna bent by this time at a sickening angle. Two days later when the truck finally came, I watched from the window, relieved, at first, to get rid of the junk; but as the gears groaned and the big wheels pulled away from the curb, I admit I had this crazy urge to open the front door and follow down the hill, screaming, *Wait, no.*

Not that I mourned for long. For one thing, a clear-sighted friend once told me, "Don't cry over anything that can't cry over you." For another, it had only been an object standing in for an object—and if some things are valuable for all time, others turn out to have a shelf life, right? But how to decide? How to account for which is which? For why I've held on to this and thrown away that. It isn't as simple as size or materials or even personal taste. Certain objects, not always the ones we'd expect to keep or remember or dream about, insinuate themselves—take on a lustre in which we are reflected: by which special effect we can somehow see, if not where we're going, where we were, and even why we are where we are. Things, all kinds—ordinary, extraordinary—tether us, don't they, to place and people and the past, to feeling and thought, to each other and ourselves, to some admittedly elusive understanding of the passage of time. Things—alone and in relation to other things—tell the stories of our lives, which, once told, sometimes (not always) release their hold— not only the stories but the things themselves—allowing us, enabling us, in fact, to move on. To keep going. To have conviction, not in the idea of a master plan or puzzle—it's not as though there's a blueprint or a picture for reference on the cover of the box—only in our singularly human urge to carry on as if meaning, regardless of notions of personal destiny, will emerge and accumulate. That is, once we hold an object up to the light— or maybe turn it over and give it a shake—once we believe it's divulged its secrets, perhaps we can more easily let it go. Not that I'm ready in most cases, not yet, to do any such thing. But it's funny to think—after the pa- rade, it was I, not my boy, who insisted on stowing the turquoise box in the back of the minivan and taking it home. Regardless of its hue, even if we'd gotten that part right, Jake would have chucked it or left it behind. He'd remembered and studied and considered and reimagined—then, at last, he'd climbed inside his creation and marched in a procession for all to see. End of story, as they say—Jake didn't need the object anymore. As far as he was concerned, it had served its purpose.

And the parade, it turns out—his beautiful parade—had given me mine.

THE OBJECT PARADE

THE OBJECT PARADE

I.

CARPET BAG

NEVER MIND THAT you've pulled your muffler up over your face; by the time you get there your nose will be red and runny and your hair will be flat with the cold, New York City cold, the kind that creeps up through the pavement and into the soles of your shoes, numbs your cramped second toes which happen to be longer than the first ones. That's a sign, they say, of royalty, although you don't feel royal, not when you live on the sixth floor of a walk-up on Second Avenue, not when you can't even consider taking a cab, last night's tips being what they were. And this cold, you feel it between your thighs, even though you're wearing tights, black, snagged just above the knee, which doesn't matter since you favor long dresses (and Capezio flats)—you with the broad shoulders and the big feet, all five feet eight inches of you, trying to be an actor in New York City and everyone knows actors are diminutive, but you will not be dissuaded. It's one of those dresses that's twisting about your shins as you walk, sticking with static, a print on fine-whaled corduroy, vines and flowers in the middle of February, which is miserable as always, but you've got your umbrella in case, and your backpack over one shoulder, the contents of which are five eight-by-ten headshots stapled to resumes, a toothbrush with the head wound up in toilet paper, a Mason-Pearson hairbrush, a copy of Studs Terkel's *American Dreams: Lost and Found*, your music (up-tempo and ballad) transposed and transcribed in the key of B-flat, three tampons held together with a red rubber band, a pot of cherry lip gloss, last week's "Back Stage" highlighted in fluorescent yellow, and a box of honey-filled cough drops.

You finally decide you cannot take another step. You look up at the street sign from half a block away—Sixty-Seventh. You've walked just ten blocks, twenty to go: your larynx will freeze, you think; you won't be able to sing those twelve bars even if you make it on time. You'll give your ballad to the accompanist with a whispered, *Skip the verse, please*; you'll pick a point on the wall over their heads (the directors and producers), nodding towards the piano when you're ready to begin, and nothing will come out.

You're twenty-two years old and you've wanted to be an actress since you were six and you're looking for signs and they're everywhere. Didn't Patti LuPone gaze directly at you sitting between your parents in the fourth row at *Evita* last month? Didn't somebody recently tell you your eyebrows are reminiscent of Joan Crawford's? You're destined, anyone can see you're on your way—today, specifically, to an open call at Actors' Equity on Forty-Sixth Street, to sing your heart out for thirty seconds for a chorus job somewhere in Wisconsin next August, but you're freezing and your feet hurt and you're not sure you should sing "Hello Young Lovers" anymore, seeing as you're not especially old, nor especially versed in the ways of love.

At this point, therefore, a sign—any sign—would be a good thing, and it comes sure enough, in the form of the Fifth Avenue bus, suddenly lurching from a block away and then overtaking you. You run, flat-footed, slippers slapping the pavement, and you catch it, it's kismet, it's your life in your face—you're in the doors just before they close.

Not a single coin in the change purse of your wallet, but you find a lone token in the bottom of your pack—there's another sign! Good that you didn't turn around and go home, or duck into that diner with the fogged windows at Sixty-Eighth and Madison; good you didn't linger to eat a bran muffin, toasted on the griddle with a lump of butter melting between the halves. You'll actually make it to the call—you'll get a number; they'll see 150 people before 3:00 pm and you'll be one of them. The bus is warm and nearly empty and you plop down in the first of three seats behind the driver facing three across on the other side, place your pack on your knees and pull your right foot out of your shoe to rub it against the opposite ankle, hoping to massage it back to life. The woman directly across from you half-smiles in sympathy, then glances away—you've distracted her for a moment, but not so she'd remember, or look at you twice.

But you—you're caught. You're caught in that face.

She's gorgeous. Movie star gorgeous. Her skin is pale and lined, but her eyes are enormous, sorrowful, set above high, wide bones. What's more she's familiar: you've seen this face before—this face like no other, this face that doesn't belong on the Fifth Avenue bus. The woman must sense your gaze (it interrupts her again)—and catches you staring; which doesn't perturb her, not in the least, she only smiles, a real one this time. And if you're pleased to be noticed, you're embarrassed, too—so you look away first.

The bus groans to a stop. A fat man waddles on and stands in front of you, fishing for change in his pockets, and all you can see between his legs, set in a straddle, are hers, pressed together at the knees, thin, almost lost in dark wool trousers. The man moves down the aisle and now you notice that the beautiful woman is holding a carpet bag in her lap, clasping brown-leather handles with black gloved fingers. The bag is as beautiful as she (you have always wanted one); needle-pointed squares sewn together, and letters stitched into each frame, letters making words. You're squinting now to pick them out . . . titles, that's what they are—of books you have read, books you have loved—and all of them by the same author; though until this moment, he was only a name, as if an afterthought printed near the bottom of each spine. Without closing your eyes, you can conjure those books, shelved together in your room—not the grimy studio that looks out on Second Avenue, but your *real* room, the one in your parents' house, where you still sleep best though you're not about to admit it (not to them, not to yourself). And that's how it comes to you—two stops from Forty-Sixth Street when you figure it out, when you raise your eyes from the bag to the woman's face: she looks like a movie star because she is one—you *have* seen her before, you *do* recognize her; this falls under the list of things you know but don't know how you know them. She's the famous actress—wife of the famous author! You'd tell her so (in case she forgot), except that she's focused just now on something out the window behind you. Is she coming from home, you wonder, or on her way there? Does she live in one of those formidable buildings with high ceilings and moldings and parquet and a view of park? Or maybe she and the author—the *important* author (a whole carpet bag devoted just to him)—have a brownstone off the avenue all to themselves.

What were the chances? you ask yourself, and what is this if not another sign? Reluctantly, you pull the wire for your stop, put your foot back in your shoe, hoist your pack and stand, preparing to descend. All you need is a word—a moment of corroboration—and you'll be ready to step out into the cold. You have her attention now: the beautiful woman regards you, patiently, and you grin back.

"Are you an actress, dear?" she asks. That mouth. The way it makes s's and r's.

"Yes! I am!"

The bus driver pulls the lever and the doors open with a hiss.

"Good luck to you then," says the beautiful woman with the beautiful carpet bag. And you want to explain—otherwise she'll never know—it's as if she and her bag wound up on this bus of all buses to tell your fortune. Isn't it?

"Forty-Sixth Street," says the bus driver to his rearview mirror.

"Thank you," you say to the woman.

"Thank you," you say to the driver.

And you're running on your toes towards Sixth, your scarf loose and whipping in the wind behind you, as if this were a scene from a movie musical, as if you could hear the orchestra tuning up behind that

Dumpster over there. Never mind that you'll spend August waiting tables in Manhattan (you have still never been to Wisconsin); that the smells of garbage and sewage will waft up through your windows straight through the summer; that the author will eventually leave the actress and marry someone else; that all these years later, you have never owned a carpet bag. In this moment—the length of a long city block—just look at the signs.

THIS OLD WATCH

THE OLD WATCH isn't really that old, not in the sense of family heirlooms. It isn't a watch at all, in fact; it's only the casing, the exterior, the glass rimmed in gold; smooth but for the notch where it would have clicked onto its back, and engraved: *Tiffany*, it said, in tiny letters, and *D. L. M.* in bigger ones—my married initials—my middle name lost to me with the gift of the watch itself. And what happened, I wonder, to its back; to the face and the mechanism in between; to the soul of the watch, a white oval with Arabic numerals, and that little knob on the side—or wait, there wasn't a knob, no, the watch worked on a battery. A second hand? I think not. Still, I can hear it. The heart of it, excised and removed, ticks in my head like a phantom limb. And somehow, for some reason, I have kept this piece of gold-rimmed glass on a ruined leather band—not the original, no, the band was replaced over and over: this is the last of them, and on its last legs to boot; its tongue curling, its seams worn to no-color at all.

This old casing, from that old watch, was one of a pair: one for me, one for my husband (his, a circle, was larger—just as elegant but less delicate), wedding gifts from my Grandpa Charlie, my mother's father. Charlie—enormous and bald—built like a stacking toy with limbs, thick and brown as a pair of trunks, and the skin on his shins scaly, shiny, stretched tight as though about to split and tear. With no neck to speak of, my grandpa's freckled head balanced atop his immense middle like a ball—sometimes mustached, always bespectacled—his eyes huge behind tortoise shell rims. Charlie of the smoke-cured laugh; Charlie of the wet, wet kisses; Charlie tanned to leather, mottled and scarred from removals of various growths. Charlie on Weight Watchers, Charlie with a drink in his hand, Charlie, poolside, but only occasionally, watching me swim the whole length underwater. Charlie in a condo in Florida—for as long as I remember, that's where I went to see my grandfather, in Miami, where he lived with his second wife (a sunbaked woman in fluorescent linen shifts), where everything smelled of heat and cigarettes and air conditioning and Bain de Soleil.

Charlie, I'm told, was a genius. Invented, says Leah, my mother, those windowed envelopes, the ones that come with bills, no need to address the return: fold it in half and face it the right way, stamp and send, just that simple. And though he never went to college, never had a music lesson in his life—Charlie played the piano like a pro, could play anything by ear, he only needed to hear it once whatever it was, so goes the myth. Except: *Grandpa*, I'd ask, *can you play this? Can you play that?* Turned out he was fluent, yes, in the standards of the '30s, '40s, and '50s. Charlie could play straight through all of Rodgers and Hammerstein; no slouch he, with Hart or Gershwin or Kern. But Elvis, Chuck Berry, the Beatles? He couldn't hear them—couldn't speak in those rhythms or chords.

Ruth, the second wife, died. And Charlie lived alone in the condo in Miami. But once I was in high school, my parents—my mother and stepfather—stopped flying us down for tropical vacations. Though my sister was a toddler, my brothers and I were, by that time, obligated to various clubs and teams. Could be while I was in college, my siblings (all from the second marriage) went back to Florida—maybe so—but I'm almost certain I didn't see Charlie between my high school and college graduations. Still, he and I were good correspondents; although my letters were

full of mistakes—cross-outs, arrows, words penned between the lines—
whereas grandpa's were clean and signed with panache. From college,
what did I write to him about? Classes, mostly. Roommates, boyfriends,
the weather. After I moved into the city, I waxed on (self-importantly)
about acting, singing, studying voice. And Charlie encouraged me: as
long as I kept up with my music, he wrote, I would never be lonely.
But now when I saw him (on the rare occasions when he came north
to us) and I asked him to sit down at the piano, it was, I supposed, for
his sake, not mine. At twentysomething, I'd outgrown him, I thought.
I knew my repertoire and my keys, and he wasn't easy in any of them;
didn't know how to use rubato—to let me dictate tempo and tone. *You
play, Grandpa,* I'd demur. *I just want to hear* you. He'd oblige—and if he
missed me on the vocals, unwilling as I was to switch octaves in order
to get through "Climb Every Mountain" or "Some Enchanted Evening,"
he didn't let on. I've only recently wondered—too vexed at the time (also
vaguely ashamed of myself for letting him down)—if Charlie wasn't actually relieved. Never occurred to me then that he'd been indulging me for
years—he didn't need some amateur straining for the high notes, sullying
his glissandos, wavering sharp or flat and insulting his perfect ear.

As expected, he entertained at our wedding: just after the ceremony
and before the band arrived, Charlie took off his jacket, sat himself down
(the sweat running from his crown and into his ears), and banged out
"When the Saints," "Bewitched, Bothered, and Bewildered," and "Almost
Like Being in Love" to as many guests as could squeeze into the room. In
one of the photos, I'm standing behind him in backless white jacquard,
hands clasped behind me, but I wouldn't have been wearing the watch,
not with my shimmering dress and my new gold ring. So when did I first
put it on? Later in the evening, maybe. Although it might have been days
before, since it was Leah who delivered the watches in narrow blue Tiffany boxes, before Charlie arrived. "From Grandpa," she said. He'd decided to give them to us, his and hers, and my mother had been dispatched
to the Fifth Avenue store to choose them; to have them wrapped and
ready. I'd never owned anything so fine and meant expressly for me—not
at all like inheriting a piece of old jewelry, this was different; a new

Tiffany watch, a grown up present, meant for everyday wear. And I wore it every day for a decade at least, as did my husband, who lost his first.

And that's part of the story: How do you hold on to something that has so little to do with who you really are? Our lives were hardly Tiffany. We hadn't meant to move west, not for any length of time. We'd grown up in the east, had respectable gigs in New York—and friends and family—and separate apartments on the Upper East Side. But two weeks into our vacation-slash-reconnaissance mission, I was cast in a play. Just like that, we were living together. The work was in L.A. for both of us, no pretending otherwise. For me—auditions, rehearsals, occasional shoots; for Fred, screenwriting—on an IBM selectric in a walk-in closet off our empty breakfast nook where we didn't have a table. We dined, therefore, side by side on the living room sofa—out of cartons more often than not, since, six nights a week, Fred delivered Chinese food. And I—I hostessed in a trendy restaurant frequented by movie stars. Our *day* jobs, we called them, though we went off to work in the late afternoons. No surprise, we didn't hold on to those jobs, though we did hold on to the watches. And somehow I believed that mine defined me. The watch—not the beat up wagon, not the tiny apartment, not the mismatched china, not that sofa—upholstered in cardboard—certainly not the bed we bought cheap in a strip mall on Pico Boulevard, which I subsequently dressed in linens we couldn't afford, horrified as I was by the way the mattress reflected the afternoon light when we got it up onto its boxsprings. As if a high-thread count could redeem us. As if we needed to be redeemed. I assured myself that we did not: though we lived in a marginal neighborhood, though we survived on tips—though we wouldn't have predicted and couldn't have accepted that we'd never know a moment of security in our whole adult lives—I (not we) imagined that I (hence, we) *deserved* Tiffany watches. It isn't even that I resolved to rise to the occasion. I was in that moment, I told myself, just the sort of person to be pushing my way through the heavy doors and crossing the carpet (so thick, so plush) at Tiffany's (the store on Wilshire Boulevard near the Beverly Hills Hotel), to ask once a year for customer service, please, since once a year the watch needed maintenance or repair. Never mind those women behind the glass cases, wearing good leather pumps and their mothers' pearls—I actually enjoyed the idea that they thought me bohemian (as if they were thinking about me at all). The thing was, I didn't need to be convinced that I was absolutely the kind of girl to wake up in the morning and put on that watch. I was my grandfather's granddaughter, wasn't I?—his first and his favorite?—no need to prove myself, but if there were, I'd have told you it was only a matter of *time.*

But. One day I put the watch in the pocket of my jeans (to wash the dishes? To water my kitchen garden?), and my jeans in the washing machine with a nice, full load. Later I transferred the darks to the dryer, cleaned the lint from the mesh, and let the machine run for an hour or so on the extra dry setting. And when I pulled the clothes from the drum and into my wicker basket, there was my watch, my wedding gift from Charlie (who'd been dead for years), shrunken and shriveled and separated from its heart. And here is the frame, a piece of glass on a band, as if time itself had been washed away, time and history and all my notions about the person I was. See here, I've put it on, strapped the twisted old band around my wrist: half past a freckle, quarter to a hair.

There is more about Charlie. There is the night before the wedding. When, straight from La Guardia airport, he walked into the living room to find my grandmother, his first wife, doing the crossword puzzle with an unlit cigarette balanced between her lips: and how she said, "Well, hello Grandpa." And he said, "Well, hello Grandma." As if they'd seen each other yesterday, as if it hadn't been over fifteen years. Then there is the moment after the wedding—a limo at the curb, waiting to whisk us away like in the movies—when Charlie rose to his full six feet three inches, and gripped my skinny groom above the elbow with one of his gargantuan, spotted hands: "You take care of our baby," he said. And Freddy told him, "I will, sir," as if they'd not just read the same script but had rehearsed it, too.

And we chuckled in the back of the car afterwards. Nervously. *Like anybody's taking care of anybody,* we said. And, *we'll take care of each other,* we said. We were wearing our watches by then, both of us were—as if

to mark the start of the thing—though it's not like I need one now to remind me how long it's been since all that transpired, or to wonder what
happened to the time.

CHARLIE'S PIANO

WHY WE'LL NEVER move again: the Steinway baby grand at my back. A reason never to move, never to paint, never to pull up the carpet and put in hardwood floors and a thick Persian rug. Although the piano breaks down, of course it does; came in pieces and that's how it'll go out; and long before the time is right, I imagine a warehouse, hushed and dark, where the experts wear button-down shirts buttoned all the way up, and wire-rimmed spectacles, and smell of polish and glue and varnish and sweat. In my mind, in my imagination, they speak in accented whispers, German or Russian (Simon-the-Piano-Tuner is Russian); they wield hand-crafted tools with grimy, old fingers, their knuckles and the tips of their nails permanently etched in black, and dark around the cuticle, too. It—that is she—deserves that brand of expertise and devotion. For now, though, just look: her finish is peeling away, little pieces of shellack on the carpet like flakes of dried maple syrup, and the action on her pedals—three of them, all brass—is loose, so says Simon, who is angular and pale and reproachful. "Some day," he tells me thickly (I only understand because he says it every time), "some day you hef money, you let me take care of piano, a Steinway, tsk, tsk." "Simon," I ask when he arrives, thinking to ingratiate myself. "Simon, may I get you a cup of tea?" "Only vater," he says, clucking his tongue: such ineptitude—better not ask the likes of me to do anything too challenging. Just look at my piano.

On top of everything else the red felt inside has turned dark and dusty—and her strings, too, are filthy and rusted. Simon tells me each time, as if I'd forgotten, that they need to be professionally cleaned and restrung. Even so, after he leaves (muttering, tsk, tsk), never mind his admonishments, his evident disapproval, I feel virtuous. I'm taking care of my inheritance as best I can and I'm happy enough with the way she sounds. She's beautiful to me in spite of the wear and tear, her rear end covered with a paisley shawl, and photos, framed, across her broad back. Sandra-the-housekeeper lines them up once a month, one exactly behind the other. I sneak around after she leaves, put things back where they belong: rearrange the votives on the dining room table, the shampoos in the bath, and shuffle the photos on the piano, stagger them so as to be able to take them in all at once: Leah, my mother; my stepfather, Ron, who has been "dad" to me as long as I can remember; my father, Nelson, who looms large in the frame even though he's long dead; my sister and brothers; my husband, my daughter, my son, and all of us together—displayed on my piano.

She is one of my assets, Charlie's baby grand, built in 1929 (a good year for the label), although, as noted, she's not in great condition, no— it'd take a few grand to clean her up (like everything else around here). Am I attached to her? Well, she's the only piano I have. A Steinway! And she belonged to him. But she's not the piano I grew up with—that one is my mother's—a splendid piece of furniture, ornately carved and polished to a high sheen; although to hear the experts over the years (my grandpa among them), its sound is nothing special. See that? The Mathusek is an *It*. The Steinway is a *She*. I am attached, after all.

But could she really keep me in Southern California? Could she keep in me in this house? Well, no, of course not; I'll go some day and she'll go with me. But imagine what it is to get her in and get her out: imagine the movers—who are specially trained—taking her apart and putting her together all over again when she arrived in L.A. just months after my grandfather's death. We lived in Carthay Circle then—known as an historic neighborhood because it was built in the '30s. So the piano was older than the block—where we rented from a woman named Pnina (an Israeli) who lived with her husband and three kids in the other half of miniature faux Tudor: separate entrances, two driveways, and we avoided each other as best we could. Wouldn't you know, though, on the day the Steinway arrived, Pnina had asked her gardeners to put in new grass—no way to bring in the Steinway, except through the French doors that faced the front yard. Which meant four hulking guys, trekking back and forth, back and forth across the newly seeded lawn (the scent of the dung in the tread of their boots lingered for hours). Pnina's husband stood in the driveway with his fists in his pockets staring at his shoes, while she screamed at him in Hebrew from inside the house, while I wrangled the team, "Tip toe, guys, tip toe," while Fred laughed on the other side of the wall.

My piano. My grandfather's piano. Which his daughters, my mother and her sister, decided should come to me, having to do with a decade of lessons; and my status as eldest grandchild; and because I used to sing.

My voice, it's said, is unusally rich, though I haven't much range; worth hearing, as long as someone else is playing the accompaniment, for what I can do with about an octave and a quarter. Therefore it was assumed I deserved her—that I would hear when she was out of tune; that I'd notice and care if her action is faulty, and whether or not her sound lived up to her pedigree. I've never dissuaded anybody. I don't say the truth—that this voice of mine, this 'gift,' is just that: an accident, largely uncultivated, certainly undisciplined, wasted, ignored, and finally abandoned. I'm not about to admit that these cords—the ones in my gullet, I mean—don't vibrate as they used to; and if the ear was ever any good, it isn't anymore. Still, I own her—she is mine—and how many people have a Steinway (tsk, tsk)? Decades from now, when Leah, whose inspiration it was to give her to me, suggests I should look into selling her, I balk.

"Why would I?" I ask.

"You need money," she says. And true, by that time one kid's away at college and the other is filling out applications.

"Never," I insist. "Never going to happen."

"I knew you'd say that," she says.

But not so long after that conversation—a year or two tops—when I send the Steinway out to be entirely restored (debt be damned), Leah and Ron FedEx checks—no reproach, no strings—to help cover the cost. In his shop, which looks just as I imagined it would, the piano-man—a pointy-chinned Russian (I knew it!) with uncanny blue eyes—runs his palm along her flank as if she were alive. He informs me that she will be perfect, worthy of her name. As if to convince me, he adds that the piano will outlive us and our grandchildren, too. Of course she will. And that being so, how not to wonder who belongs to whom?

Every house should have a piano. That's what I believe. That's what my mother believed before me—and her father before her—and these sorts of notions about how to live are as much my legacy as the instrument itself. Easy, if you happen to be on the receiving end, to spout this sort of pre-tention with conviction. As if I'd have her if she hadn't been bequeathed. But I didn't decide or choose—she came in through the window one day, along with the shit on the bottom of somebody's shoes, and I've allowed myself to take her for granted ever since. It will be a while yet before I decide, with the understanding that I am only her custodian, to take re-sponsibility. For now, see her there, her bench littered with papers and files, stacked high with books on either end: it might appear as if I never play, but don't you believe it. Give me an A7 chord and I remember who I am—that's where I live, or I used to: between the G below middle C, and up to the Bb above. Just this morning, after everyone else left the house, I sat down on a stack of manuscripts, put my hands on those yellowing keys—my fingers clumsy, my voice cracking on the high notes—until I gave up: stopped singing altogether so as to hear the train whistle in the distance, the doves in the palm, the song in my head in the usual key.

METRONOME

I HAVE A piano. And I have an old bench—came with my husband—works fine for playing; works even better, as noted, for piling papers and books (this morning I sat down on the tax returns to play). I have the sheet music chest from my parents' old house—and what a sad piece of furniture it is: scuffed, scratched, the top drawer missing a knob, the one on the very bottom losing its facing, eight drawers in between—and it sits against the wall over there, not quite centered so as to hide an awful water stain. But no metronome.

Who has the metronome? This is not the first time I've wondered: didn't I ask about it when Eliza started taking lessons? Didn't I look for one just like it? I did. But so expensive. So instead we got a plastic mechanical ticker, threw it away the minute she quit. It was no work of art, after all, not like my mother's, the one I grew up with, a solid, wooden pyramid with a brass, coded strip—not a matter of flicking a switch, no. You wound it first, then released the wand from its clip, moved the tiny trapezoid weight up or down depending, and the pendulum swung of its own accord, as pendulums do.

Back then? I hated that metronome. I hated the notation in my composition book: *Bach – p. 23 – Use Metronome!* Or *Haydn Sonata: Metronome!!* Beside the word, most terrifying, a sixteenth note, say (black with two flags)—an indication of how the piece should be played. How the piece was not *being* played. The metronome was punishment. The metronome was supposed to slow me down, or speed me up—so rigid, so unbending and unemotional—inured to my moods and my defenses, as insensible as a parade of piano teachers, mostly unmemorable, except for Mrs. Zucker, who colored outside the lines with her lipstick (orangehued so as to emphasize the yellow of her teeth), her breath sour and noxious in time for my lesson at the end of the day. Next, WASPy Mrs. Cahill—I walked to her house, just a few doors down on the other side of the Manor Club. Her living room was cool and dark, the carpet always just vacuumed, and little china figurines graced every surface— but convenience aside, Mrs. Cahill was terse and disapproving, and our arrangement didn't last.

Finally, Natalie Czerny, a widow who lived all the way over in Pelham Heights, in a house way up off the street, like all the others on Highland Avenue. I rode my bike to Mrs. Czerny's when the weather was good, bumped it up one long flight to the front door and left it leaning against the wrought iron bannister that bordered the stoop. Just inside, two grand pianos faced off from opposite corners of the room; there were Persian rugs laid over the carpet, and paisley shawls flung against the backs of the furniture; black and white photos of Mrs. Czerny, with full lips and hair, looked out from the wall and from silver frames strategically placed on the mantel. She, herself, in living color, would open the door and embrace me; then sit me down beside her on a giant pin cushion of a chaise—gold thread running through the weave—where she'd serve me black tea from a glass carafe, and sip her own with a sugar cube between her teeth. Mrs. Czerny—red-haired and captivating, managed to keep me at the keyboard for several years more. Did she dispense altogether with tempo? I think not. But she played for me before and after my lessons, to keep me hungry, to keep me *wanting*—music that spoke to my brimming adolescent heart: Debussy, Ravel, Bartók, Schumann—and one afternoon, a piece by Grieg called "The Poet's Heart," extravagantly romantic, and not to be metronomically contained.

"I want that one," I said.

And she shook her head. "Darling," she told me. "You cannot possibly understand it, not yet. Later . . . You will play it later, I promise."

"I *do* understand it," I said. "I want it now."

And she relented. "The Poet's Heart" kept me coming (and going) for another six months. Seems to me I took it home to practice in autumn, when the swirling of the chords and the arpeggios—the seasonal ache of that minor key—expressed a yearning I felt but couldn't have named. I was one of those kids full of inchoate longing; motivated by the notion—largely unsubstantiated—that I was somehow different and destined. Destined to quit the piano, in fact, but before I did, I performed the Grieg in the winter recital in Natalie Czerny's living room. Not that I planned to become a classical musician, not for a minute (by that time I'd found my calling, I thought)—on the other hand, anything was possible. I mistook my own sense of drama for depth—my passion and intensity for sizable talent. I was a teenager—therefore I imagined I could be anything I wanted, and any number of things all at once. Never mind Mrs. Czerny's assessment of my emotional range, I judged my interpretation of "The Poet's Heart" at least as worthy as my fingering, which I'd mastered, after all. Moreover, having triumphed on Highland Avenue I wasn't about to go back to playing scales. The dogwood and the forsythia were in full bloom on the Esplanade when I gave up lessons for good, in exchange for rehearsals—a role in a school production of *The Diary of Anne Frank*. Not Anne—whose tragedy I was also certain I fully appreciated—but rather Mrs. Van Daan, her querulous attic-mate, whose middle-aged suffering gave me a pain: if I knew I had the heart of a poet, I was equally convinced I wasn't old enough to play a bitchy old lady. At fifteen, I went for volume as opposed to emotional truth: pitched my voice loud and high, with vibrato to boot.

I still dream about Mrs. Czerny, who, in the dreams, is patient, at first, and glad to see me. I've signed up for lessons, but I forget to show, and

when I do, the stairs up to the house are crumbling and nearly insur-
mountable—especially in bare feet. If I make it inside, if I manage to sit
down at the keys—I can't read the music; on top of which, I'm desperately concerned and embarrassed about having mislaid my shoes. It's
hard to face Mrs. Czerny then—I can't meet her eyes, which have, in
the dream, gone dark with dissappointment. I tell her I'll be back, I'll be
better, but we both know I won't. As with other dreams of this ilk—in
which I have to take an exam in a language I don't speak, or perform a
leading role without rehearsal, or take orders in a crowded restaurant—
I am absolutely aware of myself as I am, a grown woman back in the
dorms, or in the chorus, or working for tips. And it's bewildering: is
this supposed to be a shot at redemption? A second chance? On waking, I'm mostly relieved—it was only a dream! I've escaped humiliation, at
least for now. But why torture myself this way? And if I must revisit the
scenes of my youthful failures, real and anticipated, why can't I turn the
dreams around? Now, when even Mrs. Czerny would have to agree that
I'm emotionally up to the challenge of "The Poet's Heart," why can't I, in a
dream at least, play the piece with everything I know? And why on earth
would I need a metronome? Why dutifully wait with fingers poised over
the keys, as Mrs. Czerny slides the weight to the tip of the narrow rod,
which bends too far and threatens to snap, startling me out of the dream
and back to real life—and I guess that's the reason.

DINAH'S ROOM

THE TACONIC NARROWS into the Hutch, winding and leafy, until the road starts to straighten and the woods to thin, and where before there were only acres of trees and sky, the city suddenly looms from all sides. We're on our way to Kennedy Airport from Columbia County—where my parents have recently moved into a butter-yellow farmhouse with a view of the Berkshires. We're taking the curves on a schedule, catching a plane to Los Angeles, back to work and school and our regular routines. And even so, in spite of the time, I cannot help myself.

"We have to stop," I tell Fred. "I have to see it one last time."

Ten nineteen Esplanade, Pelham Manor, New York. Half an hour door-to-door north of Grand Central: an old Colonial, white with black shutters and a widow's walk, facing out on a grassy island in the middle of the street; it—the island—bloomed with dogwood early in the year, then went fiery with maples and elms in the fall.

A year or two before, when my parents first talked about selling, we even thought we might try to buy it. (Out of our price range, but all in the family, so maybe we could strike a deal?)

In the end, we gave up the idea. We'd left New York for Los Angeles a decade earlier; had, in the interim, acquired a house of our own—a Spanish bungalow with a tiled roof. Also a dog. And a couple of kids. And a view of the mountains rising out of the haze—here one day, gone the next, as if trucked in by teamsters. If we missed the Atlantic, and spring and autumn, and winter and snow, we'd somehow grown accustomed to flowering trees, the redolence of citrus and sage and nightblooming jasmine, and sunsets that puddled and pooled across a vast western sky. We were spoiled by the sunshine and increasingly easy in a landscape that had seemed alien at the start.

"Just as well," said my sister, when I told her we'd changed our minds. "It was Mom's house. It always would have been hers, you know."

She was right, I suppose. We'd moved into 1019 in the summer of '69, just a few months after her birth and before my brothers were out of grade school. Of us four, only I was actually cognizant—almost thirteen, on my way to eighth grade—hormonal, gawky, over-sensitive, anxious. I mourned my old life (school and friends in a suburb of Boston) and couldn't imagine starting over in this foreign place; though it didn't take me long to develop a sense of ownership there, gazing out at the world from my big bay window.

That was the thing about being the eldest—I got the best room. *Dinah's room*, everybody called it, even after I went to college and moved away for good. My mother, a designer, re-imagined it over and over: it housed guests, of course—filled in as an office, and a repository for fabrics and furniture (old lamps and doorstops, rare platters and teapots)—but it was always *Dinah's room*. Once, when we were all home for Thanksgiving, two of us married with children, one of my brothers found me searching the attic for an extra pillow.

"There's one downstairs," he said. "I left it in Dinah's room."

At which point I waved my hands in his face.

"I'm Dinah," I said. "You left it in *my* room."

Was it a consolation prize, the room with the beautiful window? I'd been uprooted, forced to change schools, to make new friends, to find my balance (or not): but how to put my best foot forward (with braces and pimples, flat-chested, too tall) in a pair of shoes like twin canoes? I hardly remember the first year, only that it was bewildering and hard. I spent hours on the window seat, staring out between the branches of a weeping hemlock. From that spot, I watched the sky—read, wrote, drew, daydreamed—and spied on the neighbors. Not all that much going on with the Nicholsons—their kids were younger than I. But one of the Noto boys was around my age, which intrigued me—gave me hope and interest, until, with the start of school and the shortening of days, I made friends, real ones, and pulled my shades, and after a while forgot to look for Paul shooting baskets in front of his garage. By the following summer, my last at sleep-away camp, I longed for my room, my window, my tree. I couldn't wait to get *home*.

The year after that I flipped burgers at a local country club during the day, went out with friends in the blue light of dusk, pool-hopped across the neighborhood under the stars, and later, let myself in the back door with the key wedged behind a glass bottle in a corner of the milk box. For years, must have been, I made it home for supper; set and cleared the table and ran (if I could) from other home improvements, scarcely mindful that time and devotion were transforming the house and its people season after season. My sister learned to ride a bike in the long driveway; my brothers made a clubhouse above the garage; Ron grew tomatoes, beans, and squash, roses, peonies, and mums; Leah simmered sauces and preserves—vats bubbled away on her mammoth stove top— and stacked the jars in her walk-in pantry. I, meanwhile, took it all for granted—gathered up peppers and snap peas when pressed to pitch in, picked greens for the salad, mint for the tea, Gerber daisies for the vase on the sideboard, as if they'd always grown abundantly there in the beds under the kitchen sill.

There are photos in the albums: my sister, the baby, standing on the back steps, pointing at the sky; my brothers, piggy-backed, sparring invisible opponents out in front of the house; Leah, standing behind a stout, brown turkey (as if shellacked) on a Blue Willow platter; Ron, poised to carve at the head of a table set with heavy silver; me—with my guitar; me—with Sheba the dog; me—at my desk with my books, in profile at the piano, posing pigeon-toed in front of the fireplace, on a bike on the path that bordered the azaleas.

Then there are the pictures I keep in my head: There I am sneaking in, sneaking out, stealing cigarettes, guzzling beer, slamming doors. *Shut* in my room, *banished* to my room, *holed up* in my room—begging forgiveness and getting it for the most part, and then, relieved, retreating to my room.

Where I sulked for days when the love of my life asked somebody else to the prom. From which I escaped in a fury over this or that misunderstanding or parental injustice. Couldn't wait to leave it for a sixth floor walk-up on Second Avenue in Manhattan, and was grateful to move back and unpack myself into my old closet when I couldn't afford my rent, having given up my job as a cocktail waitress to go to acting school some twenty blocks south.

In that house, my husband met my family for the first time, and back for a visit after the wedding, he slept beside me on the trundle, his feet hanging off the edge of the bed.

It was a year after the move to Los Angeles—where we'd followed our careers—that we came back to be married in my parents' backyard. End of May and oppressively humid, the house already teeming with people, I dressed not in my room, but on the sweltering third floor, as far as I could get from the gathering throng. They heard me below (such a charming bride), panting and cursing as I pulled on my hose, which grabbed and stuck to my legs every inch of the way. My sister, my only attendant, wore flowers in her hair, and I carried peonies, prematurely bloomed because (the story goes) every morning the week before, my mother had taken her coffee into the garden to chat them up and coax them along.

At 5:30 that afternoon the wind rose up and the sky turned dark. The doomsayers sniffed, clucked their tongues, and advised us to move everybody indoors. But half an hour later, Fred and I stepped off the porch under gilded clouds, and the guests parted, making a path to the judge who waited at the bottom of the garden by the climbing hydrangea.

✍

So it went, so it goes: one by one we grew up, moved away, and came back on our way to other places, noisily suspicious of every alteration and thankful for the status quo. Verdant and sleepy in the heat of summer, lit up like a pumpkin on winter nights, 1019 Esplanade shimmered for each of us; pulsed with secrets, images, smells. We wore that house like some kind of badge—it wasn't just that we took it for granted, no, our entitlement went further still: when the house didn't speak up, when it didn't insist it would only be ours, we imagined it as helpless, bereft, and abandoned. We supposed we were as indispensable to it as it was to us. It couldn't possibly belong to another family. Not when it defined us singly and together: and how not to wonder all these years later, spread out as we are, who we'd be to each other if we hadn't let it go; if the house might have insured our bond, or if, with or without it to come home to, we'd have grown up and away from the place and each other, too.

✍

After the sale went through, and a week before the moving vans were scheduled to arrive, I flew east with Eliza, then six years old—to say goodbye, to collect the last of my belongings, to give us both a memory of her in those rooms. Leah, ostensibly cheerful, went to bed early with a stack of magazines—*Gourmet, House and Garden, Antiques*—and a shopping bag full of fabric swatches. Deep in denial, she hadn't removed a sconce, packed a plate, taken a single painting from a single wall.

My sister and I shrugged and blinked hard at each other, then shut out the periphery. We drifted in a sea of cardboard boxes, swimming in sentiment and our personal effects, while a spring rain slapped new maple leaves against the windowpanes. Before we left for the airport that Sunday, I tried to memorize the floor plan—every inch, every corner— from the back, from the front, from under the drizzle in middle of the Esplanade, holding my little girl's hand.

✍

Weeks later my mother called to say she'd visited the new owners with a housewarming gift (preserves, maybe?) and decorating advice. Capacious as it was, we'd filled 1019. The new family, though, had only two kids and different ideas about how to use the space. They'd given my mother a tour: The master bedroom was the same, but their son had opted for privacy on the third floor, and their daughter had (inexplicably) chosen the other side of the second floor hall. The room with the bay window was, for the moment, up for grabs.

"Guess what they're calling it," prodded my mother.

How would I know, 3,000 miles to the west, looking out through the fronds of a giant palm and down to the cactus below. I told her I hadn't a clue.

"Dinah's room."

✍

Months have gone by and here we are at the end of our east coast vacation—predictably too long and nonetheless over too soon. Three weeks ago we were on the Cape with Fred's sister, her husband, their kids; from there we ferried to the Hamptons to spend a few days with my father and his wife; finally, we landed with Leah and Ron in the butter-yellow farmhouse in the Berkshires. Which is lovely. But, though I didn't know it till now, I wasn't prepared to come home and not go *home*. And here's my chance. "Please Freddy," I say, and he doesn't argue; just signals and exits onto Sanford Boulevard—at which point I lean forward in my seat as if to spur us onto Wolf's Lane, then left at the Esplanade, then straight through the light at the Boston Post Road, and there it is on the right a half a mile down. The first house without hedges before the stop sign.

I'm out of the car almost before we come to a stop; hands on the hood, eyes stinging. It's blue. They've painted it blue. I lean in the passenger window.

"How could they?" I ask my husband.

"It's their house," he says.

I can't look at him. I just stand there, biting my lip.

"Why is Mommy mad?" asks Jake, who is four.

"Why did they paint it blue?" asks Eliza.

"It's their house," Fred says again.

"Blue," I say. "I cannot believe it."

"It's actually gray," Eliza observes.

"Blue-gray," says my husband.

"Oh please."

"It's blue-gray. It's not so bad. Do you want to knock on the door?"

And say what? *Hello. This was my house, before you moved in and painted it blue. I'm Dinah. Of Dinah's room.*

I stare and the house stares back. *Remember me?* I don't say it out loud. *Remember?* In the end, I have to lower my gaze—in the end I turn away first, and get back in the car.

"All done," I say. "Let's go."

Back on the highway, as if by agreement, none of us speaks about 1019 or anything else. Instead, we look into the traffic, steeling ourselves for the trip, I suppose, for the weird compression of hours and horizon that will land us on the other side of the country as if we hadn't abandoned one time zone, one landscape, one life for another. As if it were entirely natural to begin the day here and end it there.

THE GENERAL'S TABLE

BUILT, SO GOES the story, so says Fred, in some remote corner of Vermont, with instructions to make it solid enough for a woman to dance on. Can it be my father-in-law actually picked the tree? Am I making that up? Well, it adds something, doesn't it? A coffee table with a soul, an actual antecedent, *born of a single pine.* Could very well be, I can imagine it, I can: The General—I called him General as in General Mills (his idea)—standing in the middle of a cruciferous forest: *Not that one, not that one, no, no, no. Yes! There it is; worthy of dancing girls.*

Back then, I admit, I was looking for trouble, itching for arguments, but what sort of sexist nonsense was this? Consider the implications: not as though it was built for a *dancer,* no—not to showcase her *talents,* or *his,* if it came to that. It was built—according to my father-in-law's specifications—*for a woman to dance on.* A woman dancing for whom, exactly? Why, for the General himself, all six feet four inches of him; fair, tousled, long-limbed. Picture him there in that chair, tie loosened, shoes off, legs crossed at the ankle on the bench that still slides out from under my eyesore of a coffee table. There he is, a ghost, half-tanked, a filterless cigarette between the fingers of one hand, his drink in the other. On the platform before him, a foot and half from the floor, a woman twirls the length of the table and back, then falls into his lap; Romantic, absolutely—very cinematic, very *noir*—but consider: it's not like *he's* going to take a turn.

I'm out of line. I know I am. It's an affecting story—family lore. "Where did you get this unusual coffee table?" "Why, we inherited it. It belonged to Fred's father. Tell the story, Freddy." Comes the far away look in my husband's eye; there's the boy staring up at his father, not unlike his father staring up at that tree: "It was built for a woman to dance on," Fred says. "That's what my dad had in mind."

One asks, one has to, if it ever came to pass. And yes, this we know: One of his daughter's friends (how appropriate is *that?*), 1970-something, a sylph of a girl in a diaphanous dress, a *dance* major, got up and arched her back, stretched and waved her arms with her hair in her face, as if all alone in the room, as if she didn't care who was watching. Before that? Who knows. Since? Only me. Only I have danced on this table; I've turned up the Motown high and waltzed with my wooden spoon on more than one occasion; not with grace—no seduction going on—my moves are exuberant at best. At worst? Well, one time I got carried away, tripped off the end, and nearly broke my head on the hearth. And my son—we have a video of Jake, not dancing exactly, but athletically swaying from side to side in the middle of the table, almost as if waiting for a pitch or the return down the line: wearing a diaper and nothing else, performing the hell out of a nursery rhyme. All the world's a stage, after all.

What sort of coffee table is it? Seven feet long, straight along the outside edge, curved on the inside where it faces the couch; grimy with age in places; so satisfying to rub it with a rag soaked in lemon oil, although it never comes absolutely clean. But it's not the wood I mind—I like its knots and stains and scars and scratches; I even like the water rings, left over from dinner parties and abandoned sippy-cups. It's the curve that bugs me—that pretension to natural—plus the size of the thing is wrong for the rest of the room, too long, too narrow, too hard to get around altogether. I hated the table the moment I saw it. "It's a fact of your life," said my mother, the designer, who sees all furniture as rich with metaphor, as informing of character or relationship or both. So this is my marital compromise then, my for-better-or-worse-in-sickness-and-in-health: Love him, love his coffee table.

I used to have this fantasy: not that we heaved it, or took it to Goodwill, or chopped it up for firewood. In this daydream of mine, we had a second house. It was why I was saving worn linens, mismatched china, and an ugly old soup pot. Someday I figured the coffee table would move to our oceanside retreat, where we'd also need extra pillowcases and something in which to steam mussels and corn on the cob. I'd replace it then, at Crate and Barrel or the Pottery Barn—or possibly Restoration Hardware—I was going for ready-made as opposed to custom, and nothing especially upscale. I only wanted one that wasn't as long as my sofa. Maybe a two-story number with room for books and magazines and Scrabble Deluxe on the lower tier.

Easy enough, to eventually give up on the idea of the house by the water—to give away chipped crockery and a stack of extra sheets and towels. But the General's table continued to assert itself, took on new and different proportions, would not be denied.

Jake was three when I took him to spend a day at a well-respected Montessori school in Hollywood. He perched on the corner of a miniature table to watch another child do a puzzle. "Jake," said the director of the school, who, oddly, wore cherry red lipstick and patent leather high heels. "Do we sit on the table at home?" Well, actually, yes, we do, I wanted to say (though I nodded instead, smiled in her general direction, then took his hand and led him out of the building and back onto the street, where we got in our car and drove away). Yes, in fact, we sit on the table, we stand on the table, we *dance* on the table. Once a woman invited to a dinner for twelve, every counter occupied, offered to bring dessert and then had the gall to roll out her pie on that table. She wasn't invited back, I'll give you that.

While I speak of my father-in-law with a scowl in my voice, I am not without remorse where he is concerned. For though he abandoned his family (left his wife and two kids for a different sort of life), then disparaged and neglected his son, my Fred, straight through his teens and well into his twenties—in the end the man followed us to Southern California; took a place in San Diego, ninety minutes away, by which time he was stooped and frail, regretful and grieving, not just his second wife, but his former self as well, I suspect. And was I kind to him under the circumstances? I was not. I was disrespectful and intolerant. I didn't like his old-fashioned brand of chivalry and I rubbed his nose in it. I wore a miniskirt and tall boots and when he said something nice about my legs I scoffed. As if I were better than that. As if a woman dresses that way and doesn't mean someone to notice. As if a woman dances for nobody. (Even when she *does*, even with a wooden spoon, even if she isn't much a dancer.) And then, a week after he'd found his own place, unpacked, and made himself a list of things to do—*hotdogs, beer, Neosynephrine, writing group, wheat thins, golf course, Campari, pool hall for Fred* (Fred found the list on the kitchen counter when he went to La Jolla to identify his father's body)—just two days before his sixty-sixth birthday, he collapsed to the floor, all alone in that strange place, his wire-framed glasses bent at an angle under his head when they found him the following day. And didn't I despise myself for judging him; for behaving as though I knew better and more, when I was the one who'd put on that skirt in the first place.

The General didn't live to see Fred marry the opinionated girl with the nasty attitude. He never knew his grandchildren—couldn't have imagined his coffee table would live at the center of their lives: an arena for games—chess, poker, Scrabble, wrestling; a place to open the atlas, a jigsaw puzzle, the finger paints, the papier-mache; a hideout, a fort, a train, a plane; and the stage for a toddler's impromptu performance of "Finkel finkel yittle ta." Cultures in collision, lore vs. history—what wouldn't I give for one more conversation with the General? To be able to tell him, among other things: it's almost as if the table had been built for his grandson, dancing.

SPOON

THIS SPOON, FLATTENED, not a spoon at all, couldn't spoon anything, no, it's a fossil, an effigy, a spoon for a paper doll, except too weighty. Well, a mirror, then! A tiny glass with a too-long handle—but a prop, a pretend thing—no reflection to be found in its face, it's made of stainless, not silver. This spoon came from the dining room at the Miramar, that old family resort just off the Pacific Coast Highway, on a hill overlooking Santa Barbara and the sea—the Pacific, that is—that vast expanse of blue, that infinity pool of an ocean, with none of the zigging and zagging of the Atlantic, none of its temper—not down as far as Santa Barbara anyway—all equanimity south of Cayucos, at least from afar, though quirky and angular, frigid and dangerous at its shoreline farther north.

But the Miramar: faded, comfortable, worn at the edges—affordable! A few main buildings visible from the road, and then, pulling into the lot, the landscape dotted with little white bungalows roofed in royal blue. Such an odd piece of property—a train running through it—hence the flat spoon, along with a couple of forks also filched from the dining room, plus quarters and pennies, nickels and dimes, nothing but discs now, wafer-thin, their names, dates, values, smoothed away. We'd leave them on the tracks summer after summer, wait for the trains to come, then pick them up afterward and stow them in our bags—entirely worthless, inestimably valuable—instant souvenirs; better, useless as they were, than regular spoons and forks, better than small change; though, in fact, those long weekends were all about the dole every time: *Can I have a quarter, can I have two, can I have some money for the soda machine, for the candy machine, for the popsicle cart, for the ice cream shack, for the train? Will you take me to the snack bar, to the lemonade stand, to the restaurant, back to the train tracks, please?* And we didn't worry about that train. A straight line, it cut the property in two; we could see it coming from afar, left our loot on the rails, and when we heard the whistle, ran to watch, held hands from yards away (it blew back our hair and our summer dresses) then rushed in to collect and inspect the remains. An activity—an adventure—that never lost its shine, not for the under-ten set, and all of them under ten in those years; under nine, seven, five, three.

The Miramar. We went in droves once a year every year towards the end of summer—a whole neighborhood—a whole community of people. So many of us transplants on this coast, from the east or the midwest, we glommed on to each other and pretended for all we were worth until it was true: We were makeshift family. We who'd come to Los Angeles on a lark, on a bet, and stayed without ever deciding that's what we were doing; we who found ourselves suddenly ensconced, suddenly homeowners with two cars, two dogs, two children, and no uncles, aunts, grandparents to pick up the slack. Blood relations in short supply, we stuck our necks out—cooked for each other, drove for each other, stood by each other—and, all together, planned our family vacations in the last weeks of August. Found ourselves at the Miramar, where the children could wander; where we grown-ups could put our feet up, the ocean just outside our windows, fat novels in our laps, our televisions tuned to the U.S. Open. Year after year (and day after day) we lay across our unmade beds, sand and crumbs in the rumpled sheets, watched the people in Queens fanning themselves while those Santa Barbara breezes turned the pages of our books and tickled our exposed upper thighs. Up to our ears, we were, in crusts and dregs—our rooms littered with the remains of grilled cheese and macaroni and cheese and cheese sticks; abandoned root beer floats and floaties; half-eaten fruit and half-chewed fruit roll-ups. And our kids everywhere, all over the property, turning up now and then, here and there, on bikes, on skates, in helmets, and goggles; smelling chlorinated, salty, just slightly mildewed in their soggy suits. And all this debris only evidence of good health—prospects if not prosperity—fertility! Sexual viability! *We* were young then, too.

And in that place I let down my guard. It wasn't the beach that called me, or the pool, or the bar, or the sun, or the water; it was the way the hours stretched before me—unspoken for, uncluttered. Once there, in those cool, sparsely decorated rooms, the walls bare but for the occasional unsigned seascape, no trace of former occupants, no evidence of life in midstream—I somehow achieved lift-off. I floated outside the whole business, everything muffled, muted, even my own responses which seemed to come from somebody else, slightly delayed and out of synch, as if I were watching and listening—not watching, not listening—from far away, or just swathed in bubble wrap maybe. I didn't exactly look the other way—but neither did I react when one kid turned up mid-morning with chocolate ice cream all over her face, or the other put a straw in his second can of Seven Up well before lunch. I became speechless and slow-moving. It was all I could do to shake out the towels, to stand under the shower with my little girl at my knees, my hands in her scalp, absently rinsing the sand away. Cream rinse and cold cereal were my best defense, the most I could manage in my vacation stupor. Without asking permission, I turned inward, abdicated my responsibilities; a tacit agreement really—under the pretense of family time—that I would disappear into myself. But for a morning's search for sea-glass, a twirl in the shallow end, a half-hearted round robin on the ocean-side courts, I went missing, *except* for those trips to the tracks—where I could have stood forever waiting for the train, staring without blinking, willing it to come until I felt it, first under my feet, then rushing me in the face, whipping me back, blurring my vision in the instant, causing the intake of breath, and the folding of myself around the small person in front of me, or the gripping of that little hand in mine, until he squirmed or she squealed, until the train receded. Not able to say what I'd seen or felt, but I'd been present at least, there when it happened, whatever it was.

And then. And then the tug on my fingers—the clamor—the race to retrieve the quarter, the fork, the penny, the nickel, the flatware. This spoon.

MOLE

"BIRTHDAYS," SAYS LEAH, "they're boring. Useless. Who gives a shit about birthdays anyway?"

I'm calling her for good cheer but I should know better by now. I'm calling my mother to say I don't want to be over forty, I don't want to be in L.A., I don't want to be me. I'm hoping she'll answer, *Darling, you're a gem, don't be silly, you're beautiful and smart and everything will be all right.* Instead, she says, "Well, honey, I don't blame you. It's awful, isn't it?"

I'm an ass to call, an old dog to go in this direction for comfort. It was five years ago that my mother told me, regarding my looks, that I had about five good years left. It was just last summer that she mentioned, for the first time, that I should consider cosmetic surgery.

"I've noticed," she said, wiping her own eyes, all choked up, "I mean I only want the best for you, and I'm so afraid you'll bite my head off if I say what I think, but I love you, dear, and I've noticed, your eyes, those bags—if you were a teacher, or a doctor, or a lawyer, I wouldn't say a word, dear, but after all, your work depends on your looks."

Since when? Since when did my work ever depend on my looks? I'm a character actress, understand; with respect to television and film, I was never the pretty one. I'm the neighbor, the best friend, the comic relief when I'm lucky; a kind of plot conveyer, actor as device, to move the scene along.

And—if I'm honest—even those parts, the juicy ones, anyway, have been few and far between. Sure, there's the long-running role on that long-running medical drama. For which, as an O.R. nurse, I am generally capped, gowned, masked, and goggled—who'd know me if not for my as-siduous brows? To my mother I mumbled something about how I don't really work all that much.

"But you want to," she said. "And if you want to, dear, you're going to have to get your eyes done." She blew her nose, stuffed her hankie back in her satchel, snapped it closed.

"Be your own good parent," a therapist told me years ago. Which means that instead of making an appointment with a plastic surgeon in Beverly Hills, I should look in the mirror and announce, "Hey, you look great! You've been waiting for this! Now you get to play the good parts! These are your salad days! Happy birthday to you!"

At Warner Brothers one day, shmoozing between takes on Stage 11, I ask one of the regular players on the show, an actress a few years younger than I, if she'd ever consider plastic surgery.

"I don't know, I really don't. Would you?"

"These bags," I admit. "I'm wondering about these bags under my eyes . . ."

"Those?" she cries. "Those! I had them removed ages ago. That's not the same thing at all! They're not supposed to be there!"

What I should do is blow out the candles and get on with it. Instead, I call an old friend, a television star, and ask who did her eyes. Then I drive to the West Side and spend three hundred dollars to hear that my mother is right: my eyes are puffy. Fat deposits, that's all. A simple procedure and no one will ever know. I'll look rested, relaxed, rejuvenated, like my, oh, say, thirty-five-year-old self. And hey listen, while they're at it if I want, they can suck a little fat from the top lids, too. Minimal bruising. Instant gratification. Did I think the surgeon would tell me I was perfect and didn't need his services? Five grand per eye, and if I do it within the year my three hundred dollars for the consultation works as a deposit towards the full amount. The receptionist takes my check and gives me a business card. She's preternaturally thin, a Gumby-like gazelle with huge unblinking blue eyes, practically lidless, perfectly polished nails, and forty-plus year old knuckles.

I cry all the way home. Talk about puffy eyes.

When I was eleven, I cut off all my hair like Twiggy. My ears stuck straight out. My mother said, "Not to worry, dear, we can have them pinned back." The story goes that I was appalled; that I told her with more conviction than I've been able to muster since, they were *my* ears, I'd keep them as they were, thanks.

It's my theory that we girls, at eleven, are stronger, more powerful, and more fully realized than we can hope to be again until after menopause. It's menstruation that screws us up for forty odd years. Before and after, we have potential for magnificence.

When I was twenty-seven and fully a victim of my hormones, I went to an appointment with Bernie, a commercial casting director in New York City. Bernie looked at me, looked at my resume, looked back at me and said, "Can you do something about the wart above your upper lip?"

Think Cindy Crawford, think Madonna, think 1940s movie stars and a black sharpie, I just happen to have a mole, most aesthetically situated above my mouth, stage left of my nose, house right, if you're facing me head on.

"It's the food clients, see," said Bernie. "A wart right there, that close to the product, it makes them uneasy."

He scrutinized my face and peered hard at the offending spot; discomfiting, to say the least, when you're putting your best foot forward, trying to look a person in the eye and have a conversation. But clearly, Bernie wished to be helpful.

"You could cover it, maybe?" he suggested. "With make up or something?"

"Well, Bernie," I explained, "it's in relief. That is, it's a *mole*, Bernie, it's a bump. Make up can't touch it."

Even so for a week I wandered around the apartment with my index finger strategically placed to one side of my nose and just over the offending landmark. At the end of the week, contemplating cosmetic surgery for the *first* time, I asked my boyfriend (now husband) for his opinion.

"How do I look?" I encouraged, "Be honest."

"You look," said Fred, "like a woman with her finger up her nose."

So now, I arrive home from Beverly Hills all puffy and distraught and announce that it will cost about ten grand to make me gorgeous again. A birthday gift from my mother, I add.

Fred blanches, then tells me I'm absurd. Our children go to public school. We've never taken them to Europe. We haven't saved a dime towards college or retirement and I am destined to get old like everybody else in the world. The deposit was three hundred dollars? Am I kidding? Am I crazy? Can I get it back? But then he takes pity on me—my Fred, my *hero*—and tells me I don't look a day over thirty-nine.

PIANO, TOO

1.

IN THE RELATIVE calm of one nearly perfect evening in early September, Eliza announced that she wouldn't ever play the piano again, we couldn't make her. She'd gone downstairs, homework completed, and banged her way through the first ten of twenty minutes, her back to a sky streaked with orange and pink. I could have left it to her teacher to have it out with her at her lesson the following day. I could have kept my nose clean, as Ron used to say. But somehow I felt compelled to shout from the kitchen that she had a lousy attitude. Sloppy, I scolded, and I added something along the lines of how she might as well start all over again.

"I don't care," Eliza screamed, stomping up the stairs, backlit by a red sun dipping behind yellow hills. "I couldn't care less. I hate you."

She ran into her room, pulled her curtains against an eyelash moon in a periwinkle sky, turned off the lights, and got into bed.

I'm ashamed to admit I screamed back. I ranted, I raved. Not at the start, but these things tend to escalate. Hearing the commotion, Fred came up the stairs two at a time (from his office two stories down) to mediate—except moments later he was yelling, too. Gratifying in a way, that he too was provoked, but not particularly good for our skinny little girl, wrapped in a quilt, deep in the pillows, such a smug expression on her face (or we took it for smug, anyway)—who wouldn't have ranted, who wouldn't have raved?

"There's nothing you can do to me," she said with a tiny smile. "I'm never playing the piano again."

"Did you see?" Fred exploded just outside her room. "Did you see the expression on her face?"

But she'd gotten to the crux of it: there was nothing meaningful to take away, no appropriate punishment. Eliza wasn't one of those kids who cared about television or Coca Cola. (Not back then anyway.) She liked her tennis lessons well enough but we all knew that we, her parents, were more invested in organized sports than she. It wasn't as though she remembered to collect her allowance, and I wasn't about to stand over her while she scrubbed or mopped toilets or floors. "Wipe that look off your face," my own mother used to say, "or I'll wipe it off for you." But we were enlightened, or so we told ourselves, and not about to smack our kids around. So what to do? Enforce "time out"? As if that weren't exactly what she wanted?

2.

Remember Paul Fleiss?—the famous pediatrician? Remember his prodigal daughter, Heidi, who served time for her offenses while O.J. Simpson played nine holes day after day at a country club in Brentwood?

Heidi ran a prostitution ring, an escort service for wealthy, incognito Hollywood types, who abandoned her, of course, when the chips were down, when she got caught in all kinds of illegal activities. Turned out her father, Dr. Fleiss, celebrated for his longtime practice in the little brown bungalow situated between two tall pines on the corner of Hillhurst and Russell in Los Feliz, had co-signed documents here and there—loan papers, escrow agreements, that sort of thing—without asking enough questions. About the time Heidi went to jail, he, too, was reprimanded, fined a hell of a lot of money, and sentenced to community service. As if Dr. Fleiss hadn't done years of service already—as if he weren't a celebrity guru in the community: therefore many of us rallied to his support. Articles were written—and letters, and petitions—and Hollywood came calling, besides. A well-known actor, tall, loose-limbed, soft-spoken, permed his hair to play Fleiss on the small screen. Now, I suppose, he'd be asked to play himself, and chances are he'd bite—for though he survived, he suffered, no question. He lost his house, in fact, and moved into the back of his bungalow office, where, during that period, I once met him in his bathrobe pre-dawn on a Sunday morning. Paul was that kind of physician and that kind of father—willing to get up in the dark for my kid, willing to take a fall for his own—hoping, like any good parent, to ease his daughter's way, to make her happy, to help her out in what he wanted to believe were legitimate business practices.

However, when Heidi's life publicly unraveled—in spite of his manifestly good intentions and notwithstanding unparalleled care—a whole lot of people left the good doctor. He had to be morally bankrupt, they reasoned: even if he weren't, and regardless of his alleged crimes, how to stay with a pediatrician who'd fathered a daughter like *that*?

Heidi, we learned, had always been a handful. One of five or six siblings, she was, according to the commercial previews (I didn't actually see the movie), movie-star pretty and bound for trouble from the start. From an early age, we read, she'd played her parents against each other, corrupted her siblings, eventually becoming a chief executive officer with a strong talent for business. That she dabbled in drugs, laundered money, lived beyond her means, and deceived her own father was predictable the morning after. That her father, always indulgent, allowed himself to be manipulated and hoped for the best, should also have come as no surprise.

Only shocking was how quickly the women of the East Side—Los Feliz, Glendale, Silverlake, Echo Park, even Hollywood—devoted to Paul Fleiss the week before his daughter made the front pages, turned into a scandalized Greek chorus of the playground the day after. They pushed swings, distributed juice boxes, watched their children eat sand, all the while shaking their heads, wholly convinced of their moral superiority. They condemned Dr. Fleiss as zealously as they'd sung his praises, when, in the last trimester of their pregnancies, they'd flocked to him. Back then, maybe one in five couples chose a more traditional practice—but Fleiss, a Pied Piper of new age doctoring, was renowned and embraced for his non-intrusive stance: while he endorsed long-term breast-feeding, he was reassuringly unafraid to prescribe an antibiotic, or to bow to the larger cultural forces that might inform whether or not we chose to circumcise our unsuspecting sons. Dr. Fleiss was able to accommodate us all; to allow us to feel we were making the right decisions for our families, even as he reminded us that our children were his patients and they came first.

When I met him—hugely pregnant with Eliza, I somehow squeezed into the Mission style chair across from his matching desk—he told me how lucky I was. Leaning back in his own swivel seat with his eyes on my belly, he mused, "This baby will be smarter than you are, you know." And in the hospital, just hours after she was born, I welled right up when he held her and told her, eye to eye, "I'm your doctor, I'm your friend." Admittedly, three years later when he said exactly the same words to Jake, I wasn't quite so moved. Still, he'd proved himself sincere. He'd returned my every phone call, answered my every question, soothed my every worry, assured me over and over that I was the best mother for my children, that I knew better when they were sick, and how to make them well, than anybody else ever could. He bolstered my confidence and let me feel safe. That his bungalow office was seven minutes door-to-door from my house didn't hurt, but I had no intention, under any circumstances, of finding another doctor. At least not before my kids left for college or we moved east of Rio Grande. Certainly not because Paul Fleiss's private life had become front page news.

"How can you stay with that man?" asked a member of the choir.

"How can you not?" I countered.

"Heidi," she said, smacking her lips.

And I said something like, listen, Paul Fleiss is not responsible for the moral education of my children, he's responsible for their health. And how do you know, I didn't ask her, that your own perfect babies will turn out so well in the end? Solid citizens give birth to sociopaths, and wonderful people have hateful parents, ineffective parents, sheep for parents, or no parents at all. How could anyone blame Dr. Fleiss for the way grown up Heidi had behaved? And who was to say that, but for his intervention, she might not have turned out to be something much worse?

3.

There's a school of thought out there about lessons, and sports, and other extracurriculars, that advises us parents not to force the issue. Why not let the kid quit? How important can it be? Why in the world does she *have* to play the piano?

Enter Dr. Fleiss all over again: The week before our piano fiasco I'd brought Jake into his office for a follow-up on a fractured index finger.

"All better," said the doctor. "He can resume his activities."

Jake put on a face. "That means I have to practice the piano," he said.

"Don't you like the piano?" asked Dr. Fleiss.

"I hate it," said Jake.

Paul smiled at me with evident disappointment. I'd let him down. "Don't make him play the piano," he said. "You'll turn him off music. Let him play something else—Jake, what would you like to play?"

"Electric guitar," said Jake, looking up at his-doctor-his-friend, not meeting my eye. "Or drums. Drums would be good."

At this point I sputtered something about my inherited Steinway. Yes, of course, I agreed, other instruments eventually, but a good foundation first, besides which, I insisted, Jake doesn't hate the piano, he loves it, he's good at it, he's having you on, Dr. Fleiss, playing a part, acting out for your benefit and mine. I delivered my speech in modulated tones, but inside, I was fuming: couldn't we have had this conversation privately? Did my eight year old have to be our audience? *Hey*, I wanted to say, *I bet you let that slutty daughter of yours get away with quitting whenever she wanted, didn't you? How'd that work out for you, huh?*

4.

The night we fought with Eliza, Jake sat in my lap and said, "Mom, I'm afraid."

"What are you afraid of?" I asked.

All that noise, all that shrieking and his sister alone in her room in the dark, refusing to come out, refusing to eat, refusing to take her lesson the following morning with a teacher she adored; no wonder he was rattled.

"What if Eliza runs away from home?"

The winter before, the son of neighbors (ten years old at the time) had gone missing one morning before school. He stuffed his bed with pillows and crept out at dawn in a snit over his parents' response to a lousy report card. We were enlisted to look for him, a whole community alongside the police, until he was found after dark trying to hide behind a tree in a local park,while a helicopter circled above, and somebody called out his name over a loudspeaker.

The incident had made an impression on our kids as did our relief when the boy was found: nothing is worth running away for, we told Eliza and Jake, no matter how angry or upset they might be. Now, in the face of Jake's fear for his sister, I recalled their solemn assurances.

But that was back when Eliza was a prepubescent fifth grader and I was still the ultimate authority in all things; that was before she discovered she *hated* me and that she could and would do as she pleased. What if she meant it one of these days? What if she started hanging out with undesirable element? What if she turned to sex and drugs and really did up and disappear?

5.

When Eliza and Jake were toddlers, Leah and Ron, who kept an apartment in Los Angeles back then, were fairly freqent visitors. For our convenience, because the kids were small, they'd come to us for dinner, but always between six and seven o'clock, smack in the middle of what we called, straight-faced, *the disintegration hour.* My parents, however, were not amused. They wouldn't have said that kids should be seen and not heard, but they really did believe that they ought to be able to engage in adult discourse, uninterrupted, or, at the very least, interrupted only by well-behaved noise. After one especially challenging evening and once Eliza and Jake were in bed, they sat us down to express their concern. They were "worried" for our family, they said. Fred, whose parents were dead, who'd left home at eighteen, was unused to this brand of interference.

"Call social services," he blurted. Then rose from his chair and disappeared downstairs.

The next morning I reminded my mother that both my brothers had dropped out of college at least once before receiving their diplomas. That my sister had been expelled from prep school toward the end of her senior year. That I, hostage to an eating disorder, had spent a decade with my fingers down my throat. That professionally speaking, we all continued to flounder. That if two of us were married with children, the other two, each of whom had expressed the desire, were not.

"Never mind my kids," I said. "You worry about your own."

To be fair it's not her job to worry about us, not anymore. But if we're not responsible for our children past a certain point, that's not to say we ever stop thinking in their direction, right? Long ago I had a conversation with a friend, my college roommate, about the different ways we parents agonize.

"See he worries," she said of her husband, "that they'll get hit by a car, lose an eye, break a leg, or whatever. And I worry," she continued, "about whether or not they'll grow up to be nice people."

Me, I've got a foot in both camps. How to keep them from falling off the curb into oncoming traffic and also ensure that they'll grow up to be decent human beings? I don't for one second believe in the *Blank Slate* theory of human development and that old adage "boys will be boys" makes me uneasy. (If you've ever seen your kid tackled during a game of *touch* football you'll concur.) Is good and generous behavior instinctive? Sometimes, I guess, but mostly, I think it has to be taught.

My own two babies, though equally remarkable, were completely

different people from the outset. Eliza has always been largely self-moti-
vated and self-contained, whereas Jake takes a liking to almost everyone
he meets. To her credit, she's focused, fearless, and her own best company, while he is generous and social, but not altogether happy in his
solitude.

How much of this has to do with life in the womb—or with birth, or
birth order, or gender, or anything else—I cannot say. It is only clear that
we embark on predictably trying times with our eldest, now that she is
eleven and has matriculated to middle school. Catch her in the right light,
bright beaker that she is, and you can almost see those hormones beginning to brew. She is alternately sweet and confiding, then remote and full
of loathing for us, her overbearing, overreaching parents. Moreover, she's
giddy with her own grace and power, intellectual and emotional independence on the tip of her tongue. I find I am holding my breath much as I did
when she skipped along walls above pavement, ran up the down escala-
tor, or negotiated slippery boulders under a waterfall. How can I possibly
protect her? How terrifying to contemplate what, if anything, I have to do
with whether or not she falls and is carried away in a rush of white water.

And if I can keep her from harm for a time, how do I keep from driving her away? How do I convince her that my company, my love, my
guidance continue to be worth her while? Suppose, because I am afraid
of alienating her, I let her quit the piano and she turns out to be a horror
anyway. Big picture, if she's not going to speak to me whether she plays
her scales or not, better to be estranged from one's mother with a decent
musical education than without one, yes?

6.

Shana Fleiss, Heidi's little sister, works as a receptionist in her father's
pediatric office. She's in her late twenties, slim and dark-eyed, unflappable, solicitous, even, in the face of unidentified spots and raging fevers.

"Mrs. Mills," she says, as I carry Jake in from after a fender bender on
the Harbor Freeway, because he's banged his head hard and is too dizzy
to walk. "Come into room one. The doctor will be right with you."

As we leave a half an hour later, comforted that Jake is just fine (he can have some Tylenol and should relax for the rest of the day), Shana smiles from behind her desk.

"I was worried," she says. "I'm so glad he's okay."

I'm grateful and impressed. What a well-brought up young woman, I think. I make a mental note to tell Dr. Fleiss, the next time I see him, that his daughter is adorable.

7.

On the night in question, I went into Eliza's room, took her hand in mine, and walked her down the stairs. "It's 7:30," I said. "Practice the piano. You'll be finished at ten of eight."

She lay down on the bench and stared at the ceiling. Her father, standing behind me on the first step of the spiral staircase, told her to sit up.

"How dare you?" I asked, hating myself for resorting to guilt, for not finding a way to back down, for sounding like a dinosaur, besides. "How dare you treat us this way? We do everything for you."

I watched her eyes fill and her lower lip tremble till she bit it with a front tooth, white, permanent but still visibly ridged, unstraightened as yet; watched her set the royal blue kitchen timer that sits on the back of the piano, push her glasses up the bridge of her perfect nose, and start to play. I went up to the kitchen, where I stood at the top of the stairs through all of her scales and most of the Czerny, with my head pounding like a metronome, wanting to rush back and hold my good girl, and tell her, *Forget the piano, just be happy, and by the way, it is I who am nothing without you!*

8.

I worry, I do, that if I allow my daughter to give up the piano before she has a solid foundation in music, she'll regret it later. She'll resent me, won't she? For not caring enough? It's not about playing the piano, not really. It's about the opportunity for fluency—the synapses sparked, the impulses charged, the appetite whetted—it's about access, I believe, to art, culture, language. I owe it to her to make her stick it out for a while, for the sake of intangible intellectual and artistic rewards—I go on faith that someday she will be pleased that she did.

And I worry, too, that if I bend to her will, if I lose this contest, she'll be less of a human being. Not just less accomplished—whether or not she cares about music matters to me, of course, because music has given me such pleasure; but whether or not she is disciplined and focused and respectful of her obligations matters even more.

So how long am I going to make her play scales? Well, until I'm certain she's quitting for another avocation—for something else that she intends to pursue to some degree of excellence—and not simply because she's decided that the piano is a little boring and a little hard and she'd rather play Pictionary. Moreover, when I hear her pour all of her nearly twelve years of angst into Brahms, all of her mischief into Scott Joplin, playing the one or the other again and again, alternating pathos with her particular sense of humor, I congratulate myself, as if proved right about something. Yes, it's true, the human condition is fundamentally fragile and mysterious. So is it arrogance or ignorance? No imagination or too much? Whatever it is, we keep having children. We bring them into this mess with no guarantees and then we make them play the piano, read poetry, learn about art, as if to acquaint them with the exquisite tragedy that is our universal state and inspiration. Better, I reason, to have a vocabulary for our humanness, than not.

9.

Eliza practiced hard and twenty minutes later came up the stairs. We were sitting, her brother, her father, and I, eating pizza and a salad, hastily composed, since no one had had the time or energy to do better than tear up some lettuce and call for takeout.

"Would you like a slice, sweetie?" I asked.

She shook her head no and went to the sink for a glass of water, came back to the table, and sat down next to me. We continued to talk and eat as though nothing had happened until Jake nudged me and pointed to his sister, who was crying silently with her nose in her glass. I pulled her into my lap then, and she sobbed aloud, burying her head in my neck and wrapping her arms around me so hard, so tight. Like a lot of mothers, for the moment anyway, I am the parent most reviled and most beloved. And I take that in stride. When the kids come to me for all things unconditional, I am only occasionally appropriately awed. Only every so often does it occur to me that it's I who should kneel before them, fallible as I am—except that would be tantamount to admitting that I'm not deserving, which is not exactly how I feel. It's just that I want them to know that I never mean to take their love and trust for granted. But to say so, to upset their equilibrium in that way, to admit that I'm afraid I might be doing it all wrong would also be wrong.

And yet. Between sobs, Fred and I explained that we want the best for her; that we really do know better about some things; that we are the parents and she is the child; that the piano is not a punishment, and on and on—until Jake interrupted.

"Eliza doesn't want to talk about the piano anymore," he said. "She wants to make up."

We startled—and caught each other's gaze—open-mouthed and embarrassed but somehow relieved to be *busted.* And then, just like that, we were laughing—apologizing all round for bad tempers and ugly words. Enough high drama, enough cacophony. Back to the finger exercises.

GERTRUDE'S SCARF

HAMLET: ACT III, scene ii. Making out for money. Except on the one hand there's not enough money in the world. On the other, I'd do it for nothing. Meanwhile, who am I kidding, it's not like I'm getting paid—though make no mistake, this *is* my job—my vocation, in fact, and even so, there's no money in it, this is Equity Waiver: the actors' union makes a deal with the producers, and we work for next to nothing—fifteen bucks a performance once we get through previews. So why am I doing it? Because I have to! Because I want to. Because this is what I do—I love it. I mean—not the kissing part—I don't love that—or wait, I do love it, sure I do, when I'm in character, I do. But I don't.

I always wanted to be an actor—from the time I was little enough to want to cover my eyes when the kissing started. All that kissing, truth be known, was a serious deterrent. I confided in my mother then—how old was I? What were we watching? Whatever it was I buried my head in a pillow and she laughed at me. "But that's the fun part," she said. And I peeked. Not at the screen—at *her*—at her profile; her frank enjoyment.

To watch my mother watching; my mother, the most beautiful woman in the world—to imagine her kissing that way. And liking it. That perfect mouth, the slightest overbite—I wished for an overbite just like hers, even after braces and retainers, I hoped my front teeth would touch my lower lip when I smiled, that they'd crowd each other, overlap just so, as hers did. Beautiful as she was, though, I couldn't imagine her kissing that way. When my father came home just before supper, she'd turn from the stove, pose there with a ladle or a spatula, pushing her mouth into an exaggerated pucker, and before he even took off his overcoat he'd lean in to kiss her—but none of this open-mouthed angling of heads; a peck instead, deliberate and dry, lip to lip—otherwise they'd have bumped heads for sure. I closed my eyes and tried to imagine them open-mouthed. Impossible.

⚔

My friend Kitty has been cast in waiver production of *Hamlet.* "Do you want to do it with me?" she asks. "You and me, we'll play Gertrude, we'll double the role, whaddayasay?" I don't even have to read for the part, it's mine if I want it, four out of eight performances a week. "It'll be fun," says Kitty. She explains that we'll alternate Friday and Saturday nights and the two shows on Sunday, neither of us will have do matinees and evenings back to back, and I'll be home to make dinner for my kids most school nights. Plus, if either of us gets a real job—television, that is—we'll be free to take it. Armin, her husband, has signed on to play Claudius—naturally she'll work with him, and I'll work with his double.

Tony, the other Claudius, joins us two weeks into rehearsal. Thus far I've been at a disadvantage; Armin and Kitty have a shorthand, a well-oiled way of being together. How not to feel that he would rather be working with his gifted wife? I'm therefore predisposed to stutter and shake (Armin makes me feel clumsy, ungainly, not at all queenly), and to like Tony when he finally arrives. But he scares me a little, too, since he looks the villain and he stinks of cigarettes and peppermints. "How will I do this?" I wonder. "How will we do this together?" But Tony—whose voice thrums like a bass, rich and melancholy, whose command of the language is evident from the start—goes from homely to handsome in the time it takes him to read the first speech. I'm stirred.

So—am I easy, or what? Is it only because I'm relieved to have a Claudius all my own? Would Armin similarly move me if his wife were not my best friend? Is it because I've poured myself into Gertrude, or pulled her over my head? Because I've willed myself to believe I am she? Am I such a good actor? Or—is it because Shakespeare knew what he was doing, is that what it is? How much does it have to do with Tony and me, how much with the characters as written? I hardly know. I'm simply relieved to be able to go on.

I take up knitting in rehearsals. A way to be present and accounted for—focused *and* productive—since a person can knit and listen at the same time. The knitting is mindless but satisfying, the rows accumulate, un-even as they are, now too tight, now too loose, my fingers awkwardly wound in the yarn. Kitty, meanwhile, knits fluently and all the time, not just when she's working. She has taken me to a tiny store in the Valley, in a strip mall on Ventura Boulevard, where the balls of yarn are stacked from floor to ceiling in a maze of cubbies—vertiginous, intoxicating—it occurs to me, in fact, to lie down in one of the back aisles and hope for a benign avalanche. Instead, I plant my feet and pick two colors, a plummy blue and a deep violet, the pretense being that I will make a scarf that another person would actually wear. When Kitty, who is patrician and sexy and stands five feet ten in her stocking feet (we are both at least a head taller than Armin) rehearses the part, I knit and listen and knit and watch and drop a stitch and pull out a row, and then, when it's my turn to run the scene, Kitty fixes my messes—such talent—she is able pick up the lost loop and correct me from the back of the theatre all at the same time. "You're upstaging yourself," she observes from the house. "Let him grab you from behind." She puts down the yarn. "I'll show you," she says.

∧⃒

Hey, and that's something else I don't get paid to do. I don't get paid to watch. But watching is in the contract: everybody shows up to rehearsals, whether or not we stand up to play the part. Act III, scene ii: It's not easy, not at first—I'd cover my head with a pillow if I could, I know these people too well to watch them kissing, slobbering, gnawing, all but eating each other on stage—it's unseemly to watch, all the more so because I know them as well as I do.

∧⃒

High school, junior year, auditions for *The Diary of Anne Frank*, and I'm just the girl to play her. But Julie DeWitt gets to be Anne Frank. I'm cast as Mrs. Van Daam. When I see the cast list posted outside the auditorium the day after tryouts I'm almost relieved. A boy named Grady is playing Peter; Grady is skinny and short—he has pale skin and greasy hair and he smells like weed. I guess I'd rather play his mother after all. How is it—at seventeen years—I'm ready to take on a middle-aged woman; not at all prepared to play somebody just like me. This is not, of course, why I'm cast as I am. I'm Mrs. Van Daam, because I'm tall, dark, and broad-shouldered—because I'm seventeen going on forty—because I'm a character actress, although I don't know it, not yet. But in truth, I don't know anything about acting—I don't know how to use memory and imagination to conjure and transform my real experience. I don't know yet how to *act*—I only know how to imitate, to impersonate—it's easy to pretend to be an old lady on stage. To be myself? Impossible.

∧⃒

There are things to steal from Kitty's performance. I admire her dancer's walk and carriage; every cross is executed with effortless grace. The way she plays the part she's in hot love with Claudius and furious with Hamlet who is the cloud hanging over her newly married head. She's imperious, tosses her lines away—whereas I want to chew each phrase—I think if I take my time I will find the intention, find the real Gertrude in the words and in the spaces in between. I long to be able to inhabit this role. I long to be brave. To take risks. To trust myself with the language. In character, my voice sounds strange, but I mustn't listen, not to myself anyway: what I have to do is listen so hard to everyone else that I forget it's me on the stage and just play the scene.

Mostly, my Gertrude is less angry than Kitty's. In real life I'm a mother, and by now I've learned how to let real life inform my work: this boy of mine, Hamlet, I want him to be happy. I adore him, my only son. It's exciting to be married again so soon after the death of Hamlet Sr., the Warrior King, who made me feel old and weary. It's exciting to be married to a man who lusts. But Hamlet is my baby. How can I be happy if he isn't? Then, when he's rude to me, the rage wells up unexpectedly. I'm surprised by my tone. I'm stunned to hear which words are important and which spaces between phrases disappear.

One afternoon, just back from rehearsal (Act III, scene iv, the Queen's closet, wherein Hamlet exposes me for the slut I am), having put down my script and my half-finished scarf, I go looking for Jake, who has beaten me home. But, turns out, though I suppose I'm done with Gertrude for the day, I'm not ready for re-entry: when my real-life ten year old shrugs away my hand on the back of his neck with what I imagine is a look of contempt, I snap at him out of misplaced shame and frustration. He flinches, leaves the room without a word—and I'm humiliated all over again: *Thou turns't mine eyes into my very soul; And there I see such black and grained spots/As will not leave their tinct* ... I follow him to apologize: I'm so sorry, I tell him, I should know better by now; what a person should bring home from work is only her knitting.

Stealing is one thing—stealing is okay—because no two actors will play a part in exactly the same way; we couldn't if we wanted to. So long as we hit our marks, so long as we're in the light, so long as we meet the director's vision (more or less), we can be true to ourselves.

Watching this particular rehearsal—dully fixed on my best friend and her husband sucking face (I'm inured at this point)—I'm not buying it. Kitty and Armin are married so it stands to reason—very tempting, in fact—that they would play this scene for sex; but to what end exactly, and for whose benefit? There they are on their thrones, side by side, making out for all they're worth. It's an authentic performance, that's sure—even so, Tony and I won't play it that way. We couldn't. We don't know each other well enough. I look down at my scarf. I'll have to pull out these furious rows (which is what comes of having strong opinions; which is what comes of my inability to separate between skeins as well as scenes, to keep focused on the work either way). But if I'm self-righteous to distraction—to the detriment of the knitting process—I'm thankful, too, that my husband isn't an actor; that I've left him home with the kids; I'm grateful and glad to be finding my way in this part, through this play, with a stranger—a stranger who understands the nature of the work— even though I have to kiss him; *because* I have to kiss him, and because there's no taking that kissing for granted. For heaven's sakes, we're the King and Queen. We're not about to throw propriety to the winds. The court is populated. It's just plain impolite to make out in front of everybody, isn't it? Yes, we're newlyweds: but it's not for nothing that Hamlet is acting out the way he is, it's not as though he hasn't reason—we've come together, Claudius and I, under suspicious circumstances. Besides all that, look at us—it's not like we're a couple of ingenues. And, by the way, what happened to less is more? What happened to leaving something to the imagination?

Act III, scene ii. Dress rehearsal, my turn; my hair in a twist on top of my head, my eyes lined in black, my lips stained red, my crown in place just so. I enter downstage of Tony—both of us very careful not to step on my long black skirt, since last time we ran this scene I fell flat on my ass—

take the steps up to the platform and sit on my throne. I am just married and these are festive times. Although, Hamlet, my son, has been behaving in a most peculiar way, he seems to be coming round. He's arranged for entertainment, a cast of actors to put on a show. We kiss, Tony/Claudius and I. It's surprising; it's easy. We kiss again. The players file in; much merriment ensues, much banter—more kissing—oh, but that Hamlet, he's a fresh kid: in the play within the play a king is poisoned, his widowed queen, distraught.

Madam, how like you this play? asks my boy.

The lady doth protest too much, me thinks.

Can it be I am blushing?

I was one of those kids, my head—my whole self—always stuck in a book: I *was* Mary Poppins; I was Peter Pan, and Wendy, and Harriet, and Laura, and Robinson, and Jane, and Heathcliff, and Holden, too. When I happened to touch down in my own house with my own family, I wanted a story, of course. I wanted sinking ships, buildings on fire, treks through the desert, duels, parachutes, safaris, escapades, and escapes. I wanted, naturally, to imagine my parents in love, in peril, in medias res, and so I remember I asked my mother, who was sitting on the big bed at the time, filing her fingernails: *Did Daddy save you?*

She frowned. *Did he save me? What do you mean?*

When you met him—did he save your life?

She grinned. Then: *Certainly, he did,* she said, resuming her task. *I was starving and he bought me dinner.*

That's all? *That is all?*

How not to take this business of living for granted? How to raise the stakes? How to give our experience weight and heft; how to make it matter? What to do with this excess of feeling—or even just the appropriate feeling – the right feeling at the right time and place—how to make it last?

Way back when I was in drama school, a Broadway veteran, a family friend, asked why I wanted to act.

All right, I admit it (I admitted it then)—attention is seductive, and so is applause; but having to do with what? Why, with using all of myself; with living truthfully and fully to the best of my ability. With being entirely engaged and in the moment. The perimeter of my own life relatively ill-defined—the scope and the depth of my longings apparently outsized—consequently not enough to experience the world in such a fuzzy, ephemeral way. On stage, in front of an audience, life seemed to resonate with suitable meaning.

☙

On our first date, my husband and I met for a meal in Greenwich Village, heard some jazz, sipped Frangelica from great, big snifters, lingered for hours, then stepped out into the night, too cold to snow—I can smell it now, if I close my eyes, I can feel the pavement, freezing, through the soles of my shoes. Late as it was, we huddled together, our breath frosty, our shoulders hunched against the wind, until we managed to flag down a cab, which we took together uptown, where, before I got out on the corner of Madison and Sixty-Ninth Street, I turned to thank him for the evening, suddenly nervous—until he drew me in for a kiss. No big sloppy affair, but—if I close my eyes—I remember the warmth of his mouth, the way he held my lower lip between his two for a moment—I remember the fit. As the cab pulled away from the curb to take him another twenty blocks uptown, I walked east to my apartment, not tasting the cold, only the kiss. I'd have frozen the moment if I could, real as it was—and though I cannot replay it, not with Fred, I know that feeling as well as I know myself; I can summon it out of nowhere, that sense of intimacy, that clear understanding that everything is different, everything changed, no less so for having been played in real time, between two ordinary people.

An actor friend—divorced, no kids—once earnestly asked how had I decided to go ahead and *have a life*. How not? I answered. How to do what we do otherwise? Isn't that why we're determined to act? To mark those moments? To make them real? Isn't it because life is so compelling? That's the truth about this line of work—a person has to take her life very seriously, more seriously than most—she brings herself to the work, and, in spite of herself, she brings home more than her knitting every time.

Kitty gets the flu. And I get Armin. It's been weeks and weeks since those first rehearsals, since stumbling around the stage with script in hand; weeks and weeks since I took Armin's arm, sat on my throne beside him, weeks since I watched him with Kitty, all self-righteous about my own actorly choices, when in fact I've since realized it hardly matters how we play the scene: If Hamlet's any good, the audience isn't watching us anyway, are they?

Even so—Act III, scene ii—I'm terrified. We break bread with these people on a regular basis. We spend Christmas Eve together, and High Holy Days, birthdays, anniversaries, the occasional Thanksgiving. For all that, as long as I've known him, I don't feel I know Armin very well. He's gracious, and kind, but just this side of stern—I have never not been on my best behavior with Armin. How am I supposed to make out with this guy? How am I supposed to come home and tell my husband about making out with Armin? What will I say to Kitty about *making out with Armin?*

If Armin is worried he doesn't let on. Because he's Armin? Because he's male? Because he's the consummate actor, because it's only pretend, because—because, turns out, he doesn't intend to make out with me. He plays the scene for a different truth—this Claudius is solicitous and courtly, thoroughly and very believably self-involved. It works.

Meanwhile, this job. Making out with someone you don't want to make out with. Convincing yourself otherwise. It's a lot like jumping into icy water. You close your eyes, hold your nose, take the plunge, only to find that once submerged, it's not so bad. It's only a cold pool. And to gear yourself up for the dive, six performances a week, a ten week run—after a while it's just part and parcel—finally just the rhythm of your real life: get up, pour the water into the grounds, assemble lunches, get the kids to school, make the beds, buy the groceries, pay the bills, fix something for Fred to heat up for supper, show up to the theatre, pretend you're a queen for a couple of hours, come home all worked up and have sex with your husband. Or not. But you see what I mean, ultimately a job's a job.

No doubt good for Kitty and Armin to carry on as they do; no doubt they take it home to bed. Or do they? Maybe not. Having gotten to know Gertrude myself—understanding us both as well as I do—now that I'm able, I'm happy to leave her behind most evenings; to come home and kiss my husband, who catches my lower lip between his two, keeps me there for moment, then lets me unwind my purple scarf (which I intend to give to him at the end of the run), put down my things, and find my way to the bathroom, where I slather my face in cold cream and wipe Gertrude away. Gertrude—misguided harlot—carrying on with the wrong man in front of all kinds of people, strangers no less, as if nothing matters more in the world.

II.

CHANDELIER

IRONWORKS. A CHANDELIER—enormous, cumbersome—hangs from a heavy, black chain (same material) over my kitchen table. Deceptive to call it the kitchen table, since who ever heard of one eight feet long and almost four feet wide? In fact it's the only dining table we have—except we don't have a dining room. We have a kitchen. And this is where we entertain, catty-corner from the annoying double stainless sinks (try washing a soup pot without splashing, just try), across from the oven with the broken clock—this is where we accommodate eight to twelve, no problem, and twenty for Thanksgiving or Passover, squished on long, unfinished benches, gray and full of splinters. A neighbor with a standing invitation brings them from his own backyard. I take out the Murphy wood soap then, dust the cobwebs from between their legs, and cover them with throw pillows for the occasion, whatever it is.

But this chandelier, it's a hand-me-down—it's the story of my life to end up with this sort of fixture, to admire it in somebody else's house and find myself taking it home. And that's what happened. Went to visit a movie-star friend in her big, old house. Drank coffee with her in her breakfast nook, at her regular-sized table, and on my way out, passed through the dining room (she has a dining room) where a crystal chandelier hung over an oval of polished mahogany, tinkled in the breeze coming through the French doors. This rough-hewn number, meanwhile, sat on the sideboard, looking uncomfortable. Well, what chandelier wouldn't look out of place on a sideboard? Chandeliers are supposed to hang from ceilings; that's what they do. But this one—oddly proportioned as it is—was especially anomalous in that elegantly appointed room. It just didn't belong.

I stopped in front of it. "Fantastic," I said.

"You like it, you can have it," said my friend.

She carried it out of her house and hoisted it into the back of my car all by herself, lest I leave it behind.

"What is that?" asked Fred when he saw it sitting in the middle of the table.

"What is that?" asked Eliza, when she came home from school that afternoon.

Who could blame them, twenty-four arms, a black tarantula, an upside down octopus, a prehistoric bug; and nearly half those arms—generous (if primitive) loops that curved down and up again like the most dangerous theme park ride—missing the glass in their black filigree holders. The remaining votives—clear, green, blue, and amber, thick, pockmarked, evidently hand-blown—were glued somehow into the iron. So obviously artisan-made, one of a kind; picture a man in a leather apron, in leather gloves up to his elbows, picture a hot poker and tongs, picture him coming out of his cave into Mexican sunshine at the end of a long, soldering afternoon. Awkward as it is by day, at night, when the broken arms seem to disappear, it becomes an illuminated creature, each tentacle working overtime to compensate for others, detachable and removed, sitting in various states of disrepair—glass cracked or shattered or altogether missing—in a shopping bag in the back of my closet, behind the dust buster, and next to my scuffed winter boots.

Everybody was happy when I found a hook and chain strong enough to support it. When I got a hold of Bernie the Handyman, who came to the house and measured between the recessed lights, drilled into the ceiling smack in between, installed that big iron hook, plastered over the hole and lifted it up to hang it as if it had always been part of the plan.

Dinner party rituals: there's the night before, leafing through cookbooks and recipes clipped from the newspaper. There's getting up in the morning before everyone else, going through a half a pot of coffee all by myself while I firm up the menu. There's making a list and shopping—and remembering (and congratulating myself for remembering) while I'm in the store, to buy heavy cream for whipping, and flat-leaf parsley, and a couple of yellow onions, because I'm not sure I have any at home in the onion drawer—even though I didn't write down any of those things. There's starting the eggplants for baba ghanouj as soon as I walk in the door. Setting the table, washing the stemware, looking for tarnish on the backs of the dinner forks. There's vacuuming and plumping the pillows and checking that the towels are fresh in the upstairs bath—and all of that before I've even begun to cook. There's a trip down to the garden with kitchen scissors. And if the roses aren't blooming, the lantana, the potato vines, the geraniums, and the ivy very rarely let me down. There's remembering to pick a lemon from the tree behind the deck. Funny, I don't ask my kids to help, not much, and I wonder now if I've done them a disservice, cheated them of something important; that time I had with my own mother, when I was the one who set the table, positioned the pillows, arranged the posies for the powder room. But—if I'm honest—as interested as I was back then in earning high marks, I'm perhaps not as good as Leah at delegating. And though I was excellent company then, I'm inclined—nostalgically?—to immerse in these preparations all by myself. Either way, I'm somehow convinced they'll someday inherit the impulse to gather friends round a table, even before they take possession of the china, the silver, and the chandelier.

For now: last looks, they say, in my business, before the camera rolls. Then the hair and make-up people bustle in and hover with combs and brushes and mirrors and gloss and blush, until the A.D.'s hustle them out again, and call for "background action."

When everything else is done, and just before the company arrives—or just before they're due anyway—I stand on a chair with a long wooden match and light the candles.

CHICKEN STEW

. . . And she felt quite continuously a sense of their existence
. . . and she felt if only they could be brought together; so she did it.
And it was an offering; to combine, to create; but to whom?

—Virginia Woolf, *Mrs. Dalloway*

AN OFFERING. RIGHT. You and Mrs. Dalloway. Who do you
think you're kidding, you need an epigraph? You're a show off, that's
what you are. Although . . . In your defense, the quote is perfect: it fits.
It's a hopeful gesture, this party (like hers!), having something to do with
the potential of the thing; with a collection of friends—some known to
each other, some not—who will be pleased and glad, you hope, to bask
in candlelight and conversation and mutual approval; delighted to be
brought together in the glow of the chandelier in this place, in this way.
An offering. Right.

You decide on a chicken stew, a dish you know how to make by heart.
Breasts and thighs braised in olive oil and simmered for an hour and a
half, with three heads of garlic (cloves separated but not peeled), a dash
of cinnamon, a cup or so of dry white wine, a sprinkling of coarse salt,
fresh ground pepper, and a fistful of flat-leaf parsley, roughly chopped—
because it's homey and simple and delivers up a double take every time
you serve it, indicating, you think, a kind of culinary nonchalance and
grace on your part. You will serve it because it smells wonderful; because,

incidentally, it's easy and cheap; because your living room is your kitchen and your kitchen is your living room, and everything had better be done before the first guest arrives. You don't want to open the door flustered or winded or perspiring—nor, admittedly, should it look as though you've worked especially hard in advance, which might actually make other people uncomfortable. And with that in mind, you leave the sterling, stowed in flannel, in the back of the drawer. Yet you want to impress—you do mean to impress, don't you?—or to please. Yes, that's more like it: to prove yourself generous, worthy, and insouciant. You actually are all those things, aren't you? Of course you are, which is how you end up setting your table, which nicely seats ten (twelve at the outside), for fourteen. You kept thinking of just one more couple, one other person, who'd be a lively addition to your party; and now you ignore your husband's misgivings, his muttering behind his magazine, as you take the plates from the cupboard. "It'll be cozy," you tell him, over your shoulder, setting the table, placing the forks on, not beside, the napkins, so as to make use of every inch of table; everybody can watch their elbows, and everybody will have to try the garlic.

And what's the occasion, why the fuss? Well, to do with entertaining an acquaintance from the other coast, a hot shot journalist—beloved by liberals—who's been writing, since before the war started, less than a year ago, about high-flung Democrats who actually support the cause. The party is for him, whom you've met a half dozen times on academic turf: to show him who you are, how you live in Los Angeles. It's for him that you've rounded up an assortment of creative types: actors, writers, poets, painters, designers, activists, Democrats all. Boy Journalist—BJ, that's how you think of him, even though he's a divorced, middle-aged man with a bald spot on the back of his head and several books under his belt (which strains a bit at his belly)—has recently returned to the U.S. from assignment in Iraq, and is on the roster to speak at a local book festival. And when he arrives, taps at the screen door, and tentatively lets himself in (a bit late because of freeway traffic), the room is already humming, which is perfect, you think. Chet Baker croons in the background; the cocktail shaker rattles like a tambourine; candles are lit; colored paper lanterns stretch across the mantle; the scent of star jasmine wafts in from the back deck . . . a Southern California scene, a spring dinner party tuned up and playing. No need for you to conduct—someone else is already putting a glass in his hands—so you vigorously wave and go back to your salad, to thinly slicing the fennel, crumbling the feta between your fingers into the bowl. You are glad to see BJ in your periphery, grabbing for a cocktail fork and tucking into the shrimp: *Good,* you think, *he's hungry, he's pleased to be here, no special effort required,* and there's no doubt in your mind that the evening will continue in this harmonious key.

Still, it seems only natural—with everyone served and waiting, hands in laps, in the lull that anticipates your squeezing into your chair and raising your fork (*I'm raising my fork, please dig in, everyone*)—to ask BJ about his visit to the Middle East. This is before photos of American military abuses have flooded the media, but not before civilians have been killed, not before opposing Muslim sects have joined forces against the United States, not before much of the free world has denounced America's role in the region, not before we—that is, us, all of you—have been diminished in the eyes of your closest allies.

BJ, stabbing into a chicken leg with his knife, answers quickly, his voice slightly louder than it needs to be. "We're doing good work in Iraq," he says. "We've removed a tyrant and liberated a nation."

The silence in the room falls awkward and hard. Perhaps you should turn up the music? Or turn it down? Instead, you pick up the butter, whipped into a tiny blue ramekin, as if this were some kind of show and tell. "There's butter," you say. "If anyone wants it, there's butter for the bread." You've invited an Irish writer and his partner; a designer, who has always seemed shy to you, almost deferential, though her boyfriend is a party favorite, a reservoir of jokes and tall tales. Now he is silent, focused on the butter it would appear, and the designer surprises you—emboldened by wine, perhaps, and civilian outrage.

"We're killing babies," she says. Or something like that.

BJ rolls his eyes too fast—he is ready to argue, even as he pretends to dismiss her. She doesn't know what she's talking about, he begins.

The table starts to vibrate before he can go on. *Fix this*, you tell yourself. *Deflect, parry, reframe, you know how—*

"Wait a minute," you say. "Wait now, everyone. BJ didn't get a chance to finish his thought. Go ahead," you tell him.

"Why should I?" he says. "None of you is really interested."

Demurring all around. Soothing words from a friend at the far end of the table, a woman who works as a mediator/facilitator and knows how to handle a crowd. Oh, you're grateful to her, and to her husband, a scholarly liberal who reads at least three newspapers daily, and who interrupts her now, keen to engage BJ in philosophical debate. Head bowed in thanks, this is your chance to taste the risotto, simmered with saffron and mushrooms: Has anyone noticed how delicious it is? Somebody say something about the risotto, or the salad (that fennel! That sheep's milk feta!), or the asparagus—so young, so green (*Why, I steamed it with a little salt in the bottom of the pot, that's the secret, that's all, just ask, happy to divulge . . .*). *If only*, you are thinking, if only you'd asked about Middle Eastern food or dress or artifacts or even religious customs. If only, now that you consider, you'd asked about your mutual friends, or BJ's dog, or the weather in Brooklyn—you might have started with Brooklyn. *But how could I have known?* you wonder as you reach for the wine.

The designer, who has a long white neck, is blotchy with anger, her sizable bosom trembling with what she's read about casualties. BJ tells her—too sweetly, his tone too conciliatory—that she's ignorant. "You're ignorant," he says. He smiles as punctuation, adding that he's read the headlines, too. And it's his smile, you're certain, that takes her breath—that takes yours, at any rate. You know—and she knows—that she's being patronized, and she curses him from across the table, hurls an expletive, this statuesque woman who wears exotic fabrics and perfumes and who, as far as you know, only ever speaks in modulated tones. (The next day one of your guests will say that just for that moment, she thought they were married, BJ and the designer; only married people, she reasoned, would dare to swear at each other at a sit-down dinner.)

The conflict sputters and roars. The celebrated actor—who has his own television show—is leaning forward at his end of the table to give his view of the current administration's agenda. BJ, now oozing bon-homie, keeps repeating the actor's first name in the way of customer service, as if to soothe, subdue—sell. The problem is, though, he didn't catch the name to begin with; he's made up a whole new moniker for this famous guy. It doesn't even begin with the right letter. There's no fudging the mistake, no excuse to be made, though the actor, leaning forward in his seat, continues, quietly, to make his point. BJ—so gentle, so familiar—contradicts him again, as if they are dear, old friends. *You! Pay attention!* Your job now, to correct him; you, the hostess, you, dying for a toothpick, trying to work the asparagus out from between your front teeth with your tongue before you open your mouth. But the actor's wife beats you to it: "Hey, BJ," she spits. All conversation halts, and she corrects him in articulated syllables.

Now Ella Fitzgerald and Louis Armstrong are quarreling about tomatoes and to-mah-toes in the background (what fun), and your own husband—it's his party, too—picks up the slack, gives it a try. He questions the singular American hubris at the crux of a mission to save people on the other side of the world who don't necessarily wish to be saved, when so many of our own are so desperately in need.

"I'm disappointed to hear you say that," BJ answers. "Liberals have forgotten how to be liberal," he adds. Can it be he's enjoying himself? It's not democratic, he explains to the classroom at large, to insulate and isolate ourselves. "If we are really democrats," he insists, "we have no choice but to concern ourselves with the freedom of all." *He is. Enjoying himself.* He is having a fine time.

You put down your glass. "Explain it to me like I'm fourteen," you say, thinking of your daughter, who is scheduled to matriculate to the local public high school less than a month after she finishes eighth grade. "I know I'm supposed to be tolerant. I'm not supposed to impose my values on other people. On top of that, I have to go to school in the summer because there aren't enough teachers and classrooms to go around. Tell fourteen-year-old me why we're spending so much money in another country to make them be like us?"

BJ shrugs. You don't understand democracy, that's clear. "You," he says. "*You* are what's wrong with the American big picture." He looks up and down the company from his chair in the middle, then pronounces you pretenders; hypocrites all.

The mediator/facilitator takes exception. In a neutral tone, she explains that she spent September 12, 2001 in the largest mosque in Los Angeles, facilitating dialogue among Muslims, Christians, and Jews. "Please don't paint us with the same brush," she says.

Strange (though in the moment you shake it off) that BJ is without curiosity; doesn't ask her how or why she was in that mosque the day after the Towers came down. Never mind that you've brought this crowd together for his entertainment—as sure as he is that you are unenlightened and misguided, all of you unwilling to listen and learn, he hasn't asked anybody at the table where they're from or what they do.

You've begun to clear the table, backing your way to the sink, afraid to leave your guests to themselves. Oh but this is a disaster: Should you save this uneaten thigh, this wing, these asparagus stalks (so tender, so sweet), or the Irishman's salad? Is there solace to be found in the fact of his liberally buttered bread, which he also left untouched in the middle of his plate? You didn't bake the damn loaf after all, but it isn't the food that put him off eating, which is actually no kind of comfort, not a bit. You hear him pushing back his chair, the Irishman, excusing himself to smoke on the deck, where he's joined by the actor and his wife. The designer, spent, pulls her pashmina around her shoulders and huddles close to the mediator, who's argued for her better than she was able to do for herself. Your husband mans the sink, rinsing plates and loading the dishwasher. "Depressing," he growls as you open the fridge to fill a pitcher with milk for coffee. Only your single friend, the novelist, doesn't leave the table, because she's polite and accommodating—and perhaps because she also feels somehow responsible. She too has met BJ before; they have some history of flirtation, though how to resuscitate that under the circumstances? And yet. He swivels in his chair till their knees almost touch—fills her glass, then his own—and sighs, loud enough for you to hear, that your company has "bitten his head off." You pause on your way to filling the sugar bowl, to watch from the corner of your eye:

She's a beautiful woman and somehow she's managed to stay out of the fray. But something in his tone reminds you of another lecture, nearly a year ago; how you and she attended, how BJ spoke for almost an hour, how you nearly fell off your seat after his talk, waving your arm in the air, so urgently did you want to ask about his political coverage for an important journal: *What was between the lines? Did or didn't he support the war? Did he stand behind the pro-war Democrats or not?* "Good question," he said, and you flushed. He added something vague about journalistic responsibility, then went on to the next raised hand. How could you have forgotten that until now? How, indeed.

For dessert there's a warm maple bread pudding that nobody seems able to eat, they're all just so full. The mediator, a trained mezzo soprano, and her philosopher-husband, who grew up on Dylan, harmonize on a couple of folksy duets right there at the table. The Irishman is coaxed into telling a joke; incredibly BJ pipes in with one or two of his own from Fallujah. You're all trying so hard, no one harder than you—whooping after the songs, laughing too hard at the stories, nudging your custard from one side of a pretty glass plate to the other—but you're exhausted suddenly, discouraged and sad. Some of the party moves from the table to the couch; a few return to the deck, and as you clear the dessert plates you overhear BJ telling your beautiful, single, mutual friend how pleased he is that at least people are thinking about the issues, that's a good thing, that's the upside. (Should you be relieved or offended by this sideshow, you wonder? Or—Or is it just for her, a way to get her to follow him back to his hotel?)

Amazingly, everybody stays and stays. It's as though nobody wants to abandon you. *You're very kind,* you want to say. *But go home, please go home, you're not rats, and anyway this ship already sank.*

At last, on his way out the door, BJ takes your hand. "I don't want you to feel bad," he says, all benevolence. "Please don't upset yourself about what happened tonight." He kisses your cheek. He insists that he hopes you will keep in touch.

In the moment, you're stunned to silence—as if trying to remember your lines. You hadn't seriously supposed any of this to be your fault;

but was it? Is it? As if cued, you nearly apologize, then catch yourself and improvise to wish him a safe trip home instead. It's not as if you could have prevented the debacle, right? It was an offering; you only wanted everybody to try the garlic and to have a good time.

We're at war, you tell yourself as you blow out the candles. *Away and here at home, we're at war.* "Even if we weren't . . . ." you mumble aloud; even at your own dinner table, it's becoming more difficult to recognize friends, enemies, casualties, too, for who they are. Meanwhile, there are empty bottles, wine-stained napkins, burned out candles, ice in a puddle, crumbs scattered across the floor, a sink piled high; nothing to do but clean it all up, put it all away. You plop down on a chair at the table, smear a piece of garlic across a hunk of bread. Chew and swallow, then get up again to search for a container under the counter, something big enough to hold the leftover chicken—which, according to the recipe, is actually supposed to taste better tomorrow.

NESTS

STILL DARK, THE alarm not yet sounded, that lumpy silhouette of a clock still comatose, when the bird band begins to tune up, tentative at first, and then full-tilt cacophony, like any orchestra. I like to imagine they summon the light, knowing before we do that the sun is hiking up behind that hill to the east. Of course it's an accidental score—except there are no accidents, or there are only accidents, depending on your spiritual persuasion. Either way, the sun will rise and the birds will seem to serenade her from our trees—from their nests in the palm, the eucalyptus, the liquid amber, the Chinese elm—such a riot of chirping, whistling, cawing; never louder, never more insistent than now as the sky goes from amethyst to opal to the whitest Southern California blue. And under and over it all—weaving, punctuating—the mourning dove. An oboe, or is she a clarinet? How is it I never noticed her in childhood? And how is it she's haunted me these last two decades, a feature of my grown up life—crow's feet at the corners of my eyes, that dove's song in my ears—but surely she was there all along, this Klezmer soloist, this Jewish mother of a bird. Get a job, a job, a job, she warned straight through my twenties; what's for dinner, dinner, dinner, she's nagged since my children were old enough to ask; and now that one is ready to fly the coop and the other keeps his own confidence more often than not, her lament is more philosophical: what's it all for, for, for.

⚘

Group therapy in the desert. Sixteen chairs, three families, eight people arranged in a circle, we can move around for a better view of the action in the center if we like, and right now the players are my mother and my sister; a therapist on his knees on the floor beside them, from where he prods and provokes and occasionally reminds them of the rules.

How old do you feel? He asks my sister.

"Fourteen," she admits, for starters.

Moments later, *How old now?* Like a game show contestant, squinting, stammering, hoping to win the whole pot, she ventures, "Um . . . Twenty-nine?"

Finally, the third time he asks, she answers with huge resolve. "Thirty-four."

She's thirty-six, in fact, growing up on the spot, you have to stare hard, like watching crocus in the spring. No judgment here—I've no idea myself, how to act or feel as old as I am.

Afterwards, we in the outer circle get to have our say. What did we observe—how do we identify (if we do)? My brother Joe goes first. He sees, he offers, a beautiful bird in a gilded cage full of shit.

In the break, we walk out of the low building and into clean Arizona sunshine, a watercolor sky. The heat rises off the paved path, shimmers and hovers; wooden benches sit under trees heavy with lemons and tangerines, and the grass is clipped and uniformly green; birdsong above. *Why are we here (here, here),* croons that dove, and I don't doubt she's followed me all the way to Tucson. Jill goes off to smoke, as does Joe, but separately, not together. Ron sits down on a wooden bench, examines the cactus and his fingernails, and my mother and I end up side by side at the sinks in the restroom, washing our hands.

"Come on," I say, "A bird in a gilded cage? This is an original thought . . . ?"

"A gilded cage full of *shit*," chortles my mother, "I think it's a wonderful metaphor, I really do."

✍

Just weeks before, I'd flown into Tucson from L.A. a couple of hours before my sister arrived from New York. She'd been released from Mount Sinai and escorted to Kennedy Airport on the condition that a family member meet her to check her into a full-time rehab facility. She let me hug her when she got off the plane, but she couldn't look me in the eye. Her skin was pale, lips chapped, hair in need of cutting, eyes downcast as if her upper lids were too heavy somehow. When she glanced in my general direction, I saw that the whites were yellowish and shot through with tiny red veins.

In the cafeteria, after she'd filled out her paperwork and before I caught my ride back to the airport, my sister unwound the gauze from her wrists, coiled each long strip on one forefinger, and then left the twin spools in a corner of her tray. I reached for her hands and she turned them to fists in my grasp.

"Let me," I said.

"No."

"Let me see," I said again and she opened her palms, and looked up at the ceiling.

I kissed each wound, but the gesture was flat, the moment forced and false—perhaps because I'd allowed myself to imagine it. Jill pulled her hands away. Jammed them in her lap between her thighs.

When I arrived home that evening, I found a dove trapped in my office, adjacent to the master bedroom. We scared the crap out of each other. She trembled in a far corner, under the hand-me-down baby grand with the peeling finish. Fred, my husband, got a broom, opened the sliding glass doors, shooed her in the direction of the deck. The brush of bristles against the ivories, the brush of wings against the curtains, tripping, shrieking, grunting, a confusion of flapping, and she was gone. The next morning bird shit octave to octave, sticking between the keys. And from an undisclosed location in the backyard came her apology. Or was it another reprimand? An indirect, my husband calls it, when a person says, I'm sorry, but it's all your fault.

Jill and Leah, my sister and my mother, face each other in chairs. Leah gestures as she speaks, makes circles in the air, her fingers move independently of each other. She loves us all, she insists, equally and differently—the consonants articulated, the vowels pronounced just so—but Jill, her baby, her sidekick, her companion in her dotage (she doesn't say that), she cannot imagine a life without Jill, life wouldn't be life; life would be nothing. *Am I allowed to tell her that?* She breaks off to ask, her voice suddenly squeezed high in her throat, *Am I allowed to put this kind of pressure on her?*

Slumped in his chair beside me, Ron's shoulders are shaking. He makes odd little noises, as if he is having a nightmare. I put my hand on his arm half-expecting him to shrug me away, but he doesn't. Just trembles, you could mistake this for laughter, these sounds he cannot suppress, except his cheeks are wet.

Jill—my middle-aged sister—believes she is a burden, *a mistake*, not news to her, not news to any of us, my mother was meant for better, never wanted a fourth child.

"But once I saw you, once they put you in my arms, I fell in love, how not?"

Leah says. "You have to understand," this to the room at large, "I was a feminist. I didn't want another baby. Fifty years I've given to motherhood, I'm sick to death of it, and, mind you, all this was long before Roe v. Wade . . ."

Later Joe says, "Mom, you can't talk about Roe v. Wade anymore, do you get that?"

We are sitting in the hotel lobby, happy hour, and we're dissecting the events of the afternoon. Four weeks into Jill's therapy, three days into family week—an institution unto itself—we're shouting at each other above the din, the sofa and chairs too deep, too far apart, we've thrown propriety to the winds.

"But I never resented Jill, I was angry with Daddy," hollers my mother, as though he isn't right there, sitting right beside her in a big club chair with his hands in his lap and his chin on his chest.

Is he sleeping? I stare at him. I start to laugh and cover my mouth. He opens his eyes on a snort, folds his arms across his chest, smirks and says nothing.

"He wouldn't look at me," Leah continues. "He wouldn't talk to me. I'd been diapering babies since I was twenty years old but the idea that I'd want to get rid of a baby of ours . . . He was outraged."

My stepfather grimaces and shakes his head. He mutters something to the space in front of him.

Leah sniffs, reaches into her black satchel for her lipstick, applies the color and blots her mouth with the paper cocktail napkin from her drink.

⚅

Handcuffs: On the one wrist coral beads, many strands, a thick braid of them tightly woven and clasped. On the other, two wide lavender bands: leather? Vinyl? Flat, sterling envelopes where the watch faces would be, inside each envelope, a silver wafer of a message, engraved with words of hope and abstinence.

My sister wears these always; doing the crossword at the kitchen table; in a clinch with the dog under the kitchen table; smoking a cigarette outside after dinner, she has pulled the sliding doors closed to keep the smell from coming in the house. She's with us in L.A. for an indeterminate spell. I picked her up at the airport two days ago, post-family therapy in Tucson, en route to a residential second-phase facility in Laguna Beach. She was to stay with us only one night, didn't even unpack her overstuffed duffel, blue and rose chintz with leather handles. The following morning we found the halfway house in Laguna, indistinguishable from its neighbors, a bungalow with a narrow, brown front porch and a narrow, brown front lawn. I took her to lunch around the corner, then checked her in, helped her bring her bags into a tiny room with one closet and metal bunk beds; the top cot tightly made with sheets and matching pillowcase covered in big pink hearts—a long crack in the ceiling, a flimsy, stained shade hanging askew across a small high window, and on the wall a list of mandatory chores and meeting times.

"I'll be all right," she promised, wiping her eyes, not watching me go.

"Call me," I said.

And she did. Less than two hours later I was on my way back to Laguna in bumper to bumper, and an hour after that I found her sitting on the curb—leaning against her duffel, elbows on her knees, chin in her hands.

⚹

Jill spends the next few days researching the alternatives, trying to find the right fit, it's not the idea of bunk beds she minds, but that schedule on the wall, those mandatory meetings, she can do without them.

"I could just go home," she ventures, "I could just go home to Roy."

Roy this, Roy that. Roy is her lover, who lives up the road from my parents' weekend retreat in Columbia County, in the Berkshires, very near the Massachusetts state line. It's as though Roy is her tether, proof of her worth and existence on this earth; she is loved, see, she's a grown woman with a lover, lest we forget, and also a dog. Roy will take Barney while I'm away, she repeats, in case I've forgotten, as if Barney was a child, as if I'd asked to be his guardian, myself. *I'm all grown up,* is the message, *I have a lover, I have a dog, I have a life! Pinch me, I'm real.*

⚹

Roy met my sister at a neighborhood barbecue last summer.

She went to the party with my parents.

He went with his wife.

Who supports him because he took early retirement.

Who has no intention of letting him out of the marriage.

My mother says Roy has had multiple affairs. My stepfather says Roy can't keep his pecker in his pants.

My mother says Jill is not the first of Roy's casualties. My stepfather says he won't support Roy in the manner to which Roy has become accustomed.

She seems to have forgotten that Jill only slit her wrists *after* she broke it off with Roy. *He* seems to have forgotten *he himself* insisted she end the affair.

What bothers them most about Roy? That he's married? That he lives down the road? That he has grandchildren? Is it the idea that he would move in with Jill, who charges clothes and haircuts and occasional toiletries to daddy's American Express?

"Jill is almost forty years old," said the psychiatrist at Bellevue, when my stepfather questioned his daughter's right to doctor-patient confidentiality.

"That doctor," he says, "she doesn't care about Jill! She doesn't even know how old she is! She's only thirty-six!"

"Roy has a reputation," says my mother. "He preys on young women."

"She's not that young," I say, as if they can hear me.

"We had a haven here," my mother says, "We had a place to go, to be ourselves, and your sister went and pooped all over it."

Yellow with white shutters, set among the trees, and from the eaves in each corner of the wide green wrap-around porch hangs a birdhouse and the birds are abundant, come and go as they please, as does my sister, who has a room on the second floor, her books on the shelves, her clothes in the drawers; how dare she grow up? How dare she make a mess of things here, in her parents' house? Gilded as it is, how could she have known it for a cage?

We're socked in, we've been socked in for days, the mountain range to the north has disappeared as if rolled away like a Hollywood set. The script supervisor at the studio in Whittier, where I'm working as a guest star on a television show, confides he keeps parrots, five of them. "They're just like kids," he says and to prove it he puts his cell phone to my ear.

"Hello Daddy," cracks one of the birds.

"He's upset," says the script supervisor after he hangs up. "He hates it when it's overcast."

"What's with this weather?" asks my sister when I arrive home from the set. She came to California with an assortment of short shorts and bikini tops and bottoms. She wears madras flip flops. Her toenails are painted red and she has a purple pansy tattooed on the inside of her right ankle. She observes, folding laundry out of a big wicker basket on my kitchen table, that my underwear is boring. You need variety, she remarks. For one thing, it'd be easier to organize in my drawers according to color and pattern. For another, stripes, polka dots, flowers, they'll give me a lift; according to her, they'll cheer me right up.

Meanwhile, she muses, *she's* going to adjust her medication, but not before she gives daylight savings a chance. It unnerves her—like everyone else, she adds—to wake in the dark. She disappears into the garden to have a smoke.

The dove must be hiding in the palm, not far from where Jill sits folded like origami with her chin up against her knees. *What's with this weather?* calls the dove three times from deep inside the fronds.

Later, we walk the loop in the wilderness adjacent to Dodger Stadium, where the birdman of Echo Park erects his sculptures in the eucalyptus trees, now pungent and aggressively molting. The brush is tangled and dry and noisy with bushtits, and the long grass is beginning to go brown on both sides of the path. Up ahead, there's a murder of no-necked crows, oversized and so black it's as though they haven't eyes. Hunched in a line along a high branch, they whoosh away as we approach, reluctantly, with a great and caustic squawking. Above them, the birdman's eagle is poised for flight, still as the tree—stiller—taunting us who are alive and fearful.

"Tell me if I'm not supposed to ask you this," I begin. "But if you love Roy, if you're in love, how could you have wanted to die?"

"He asks me the same thing," Jill answers. "He asks how he didn't know this about me. And I tell him, nobody knew. Nobody."

Who isn't unhappy? But my sister—she's more than unhappy, she's something else. She's exhausted. She's been such a good girl for such a long time, she's done all the right things, and for what? For whom? How did she wind up lonely enough—desperate and angry enough—to turn away from her own fine-boned reflection in the bathroom mirror, to sit down on the side of the tub and take a razor to her wrists, delicate, olive-skinned, and smooth? Didn't do her research, cut on the horizontal instead of the vertical, and she didn't succeed. An accident? Or does it mean she didn't want to? When I wonder out loud, she sets me straight: she meant it all right. It's just that it's extremely hard to do it right.

Turns out I had it wrong, all wrong. Turns out—according to ornithologists—that my dove, the one who's been following me all these years, is male. He's not following me. He's wooing his female counterpart.

Wooing her and wooing her and wooing her over and over and over again. His song isn't meant for me at all.

"Do you know Roy?" asks Jake.

I tell him I don't.

But he does. He remembers the neighbor down the road from his grandparents who got wind of Jake's annual visit last summer and offered to take him kayaking. He remembers that Jill went along for the ride. And Jill has only just confided—when I asked how she and Roy got together—that she left her sandals in the back of the truck that afternoon, skipped up the lawn in her bare brown feet when Roy dropped her and Jake back at the house; an excuse to call and make plans to see him again.

"What do you think about him?" Jake persists.

"I don't," I say again.

"Really, Mom . . ."

"I don't think about him," I say. "It's none of my business."

But this is what my mother said to *me*—about a succession of boys, of men—right up until the day I was married. "I have no opinion, Dinah, this is your choice," said she, with evident pride in her neutrality. And I mistook that pride for disapproval every time; why else withhold her blessing?

I've gone out back to water the roses, to deadhead the geraniums, to trim the lantana, cut basil for my panzanella, when I see my dove. It's her, it must be, perched on the railing, watching me with my hose and my clippers; how long has she been there, not a peep, not a word, but I recognize her—discreetly speckled, demure, *significant*—and I'm certain she knows me too.

How we cowered, we two, in opposite corners of a room full of furniture; but out here I can't get close enough. I'm unafraid, as is she, or at least that's what I believe until I take a step in her direction. She flies then, rises into the thick of the Liquid Amber, budding with green, only a few red leaves still clinging to its branches. I can't see her there, but I will her to call to me—I could do with a little chiding just now, an indication that she cares, she's invested, that we're somehow in sync.

Yes, I realize, I remember, she is a *he*, or if she is a *she*, *she* hasn't been singing, *he's* the singer, and he's been singing to *her*, not me, but never mind all of that. I'm looking—listening, that is—for a sign.

A few days until Jill is scheduled to leave L.A., and to her credit we are only just now beginning to bump into each other; too many towels in the laundry, too much hair in the shower drain, not enough room on the couch to sprawl with my book; but we can manage for a few more days.

Eliza calls to me from her corner of the house, figures it out, and trips down the stairs to find me reading in the middle of the big bed.

"Mom," she demands from the doorway, "can I ask you something?"

"You bet."

She takes a step into the room. Her voice gets young and small. She wants to know if Jilly cuts herself.

I close my eyes. I open them again.

"I saw her wrists. Like Danny's, that kid who sat next to me in orchestra. Except scars not scabs. Is she a cutter, Mom?"

"I guess she must be," I answer.

Eliza stares me down. "Mom, did Jilly try to kill herself?"

"I guess she did."

She almost stamps her foot.

"What else haven't you told me?" Full-voiced now, she's asserting all of her sixteen years.

"It isn't my business to tell you," I say, "I've told you as much as Jill wanted me to tell."

How feeble I am. Upstairs I put on a kettle for tea and enter Jake's room, where Jill is playing solitaire at the computer. I sit down on the bed.

"Eliza saw your wrists."

Her eyes fill. She is so sorry.

"Don't be," I say, "I don't want you to be sorry. But I want you to talk to her before you go."

In a whisper, I tell her I want her to say she's glad to be alive; it was all an accident, an awful mistake.

Jill nods vigorously, "Of course."

Of course, of course.

I'm remembering a visit with a friend, how not so long ago we sat in her kitchen in the waning light of a winter afternoon. Smack in the middle of the table, a centerpiece she'd taken home from a luncheon the day before, leaves and berries arranged in a glass bowl, and sticking up out of the middle, fastened to a plastic stem, calligraphy on cardstock, Louise Gluck's "The Night Migrations," the image of birds flocking in a dark sky. While my friend made coffee, I sifted the words over and over, stunned by the revelation in the second stanza. Such witnessing—the beauty of birds in flight—is only for the living. I want those words engraved on a sliver of silver, better yet tattooed to my sister's ankle in place of that pansy: ... *the dead won't see them –/ These things we depend on, they disappear./ What will the soul do for solace then?*

✍

My daughter is a pole vaulter. She's all limbs, all legs and arms and a long fiber-glass pole, it bends under her weight and she soars up and flips over, turns in mid-air. Sometimes she misses, knocks the bar off on the way up or the way down, sometimes she falls, skins a knee or an elbow, and sometimes she sails right over, *Look Ma, no wings.*

One time, she trips before she plants her pole and turns her ankle. I see the hurt in her eyes, but her coach is on her right away, teasing, merciless, "Don't run like a girl," he yells, prancing down the track and waving his arms. She jumps up and laughs back at him, prances herself, dances back to her place in line, only catches my eye for a moment, and then looks away as if to say, don't come to me, don't talk to me, don't feel sorry for me, don't, don't, don't. A few weeks later, she gallops down the runway again and again, knees high—long, even strides.

"Good run!" the coach shouts, jubilant, even after she knocks the bar off at eight feet.

But the skinned knee, the twisted ankle, the grimace of pain, is nothing to the invisible wound; the sobs come unchecked and convulsive, when she cannot break her own record at city finals, can't even meet it, and somebody else can.

Afterwards, in the car, she presses herself against the passenger door, her nose to the glass, cuts me off when I offer words. I can't fix it anymore, I'm only her mother, bewildered more often than not by the damage I cannot prevent or contain. She doesn't want to talk, she wants to get away, from here, from me. Though I've abandoned the afternoon freeway traffic for the streets—though ordinarily we'd stop for a slice at Hard Times in Los Feliz, or at least a cold drink—close as we are to home neither of us makes the suggestion.

As always, a long row of pigeons on the wire over the red light at Hyperion; just before it changes, just before I take the right onto Rowena into Silverlake, heading towards the hills of Echo Park, they rise as one, swoop this way and then that, aerial maneuvers, perfectly choreographed and executed, and then they fly off all together, all in the same direction, as if with purpose and aforethought.

Out back, a sparrow—I could hold her in my palm—hits one of the sliding doors with a thud. Birds slam into windows at high speeds; something to do with reflection—they can't parse it. Though their eyes are better than ours, though they see colors we can't begin to imagine, it doesn't occur to them to look beyond the sky in the glass. If they're lucky, if they catch a glimpse of themselves on the wing—they're less likely to die; deceived either way, but at least they know enough to slow down, to be wary of the enemy in the mirror. Which must have been the case with this stunned, little creature; she lies on her side, breathes fast and hard until she puffs herself up to standing, and when I check again before I let the dog out, sure enough, she's gone.

Jill, meanwhile, is on her way back to New York from a halfway house in Florida. She lasted scarcely three months out of the prescribed six, but in the end, she explains on the phone, the program wasn't for her. She wants her life back, that's what she wants, so she's going home to the yellow farmhouse with the white shutters, moving in with our parents, who have agreed to help her get her bearings, so long as she promises not to see Roy. They're magnanimous. Forgiving. But what's to forgive? I imagine her there, working in the garden with her father, putting up preserves with her mother; framed like a picture in the second story window.

⚜

Those doves? Year after year they build their nest in the bougainvillea adjacent to the front stoop. One morning, a broken egg on the path, still wet, a bit of yolk, pale yellow, clings to the fractured shells.

Back in the nest, buried deep in the bush, persistent peeping, and when we open the front door the rush of wings, the mother hovers at attention over there in the wisteria, bird shit all over the stucco wall beneath the trailing branches and blossoms. I sweep away the bits of white and yellow, but I'll wait until the birds vacate for good—all of them—before I take out the hose and the house paint.

⚜

A weekend morning, Jake's eating breakfast, making crumbs all over the sports section, when all of a sudden he looks up from the paper.

"Mom," he says, with his mouth full of toast. "Listen to that bird."

"The dove?"

"The one that has to say everything three times."

"The mourning dove," I say.

"She's talking to me," says my son.

"She's a he," I tell him.

Jake gets up from the table, takes his plate to the sink. "She's been following me around my whole life, she's driving me crazy."

"But you realize, it's not the same bird, honey, it's a different bird every year, you know that, right?"

I mean to be of comfort—but he shakes his head and makes for the front door on his way who knows where. And just before he lets the screen slam behind him, he says, "And that's where you're wrong."

COLLAR

THIS CIRCLE OF dirty red canvas and nylon hangs from a hook on a mirror in the bedroom, alongside a couple of baseball caps and Gertrude's plummy scarf. An inch wide, a quarter-inch thick, buckled on the first of four holes, heavy duty and over-sized. Fred brought it home the day we left her at the vet to be cremated, and retrieved (in a box) a week or so later. And here's the thing: it smells of her—of Roxy, our first dog—a chocolate Lab with a narrow head, the last of her litter, so tiny when Fred picked her up at the Labrador farm in Sierra Madre that she nearly fell between the seats in the Beast (our old wagon) before he got her home. This is her collar, removed eleven years later and still faintly sour: that odor, greasy and rotten, foul and sweet—it used to stick to my fingers, I remember; poor thing, she suffered in the heat.

And I suffered, too—held my nose and made faces and begged Fred to bathe her. Which he did. Soaked her with a cold hose in the front yard and lathered her up in the street. She stood there, head hanging, feet planted in the gutter, braced against the water rushing down Princeton Avenue, facing downhill—in spite of our efforts to turn her around, so as to keep the soap from running into her eyes. After he dried her off, he'd tie the towel around her head like a babushka; and she'd pose for a moment, forlorn, bewildered, as if straight off the boat (from the shtetl)—a William Wegman plus-size model. Then she shook off the towel and shook herself out; superdog in reverse; revived and revved up, she ran circles in a frenzy, spraying water this way and that, although it took her hours to really dry, so thick and oily was her coat.

But this collar—coated with dust inside the buckle, and three tags hanging from a ring near the last notch: the first, tinted orange, from the Los Feliz Small Animal Hospital; next, her permanent license (from Animal Regulation, City of L.A.); and the third—a perfect disk worn smooth and dull and difficult to read—our last name and address on one side; *Roxy* (the X rubbed to nothing but a backwards slash) and our phone number on the other.

Roxy. How did we pick her name? Now I am tired of diminutives —of dog-*gies*-tired of my own voice shouting for this old boy (Sully: Fred's choice) who will loiter and roll in something dead if he gets the chance— and this pup (Elphie—short for Elphaba, the name with which she came to us), who runs ahead into the tall grass only to reappear with foxtails buried between her tufted toes and in that extra hair hanging off of her ears like payos. But Roxy—we came up with it together because we liked Sting, for one thing—and because we didn't have children, not yet, and it wasn't a name we'd have held in reserve for a girl. And how did we decide we wanted a dog in the first place? It had something to do with growing up with them, both of us, and with buying the house—our first. Something to do with us as newly married; with three bedrooms, two baths, and a big backyard (but with only a couple of toes in that water, not all four feet, not yet); and something to do with announcing that we really and truly lived in California. Weren't going home (back East, that is) any time soon.

Fred, fixed as he was on the breed, combed the Classifieds and located a litter less than an hour to the east. No question he'd come home with a dog—how do you visit a bunch of puppies and not bring one home? Although by the time he got there, only Roxy was left, who knows why?

The smallest, we figured later on, plus her head wasn't as square as most: a bit pointy in the nose, Roxy was, such is the privilege of pedigree—features that end in a point. She came with a rag, a piece of burgundy towel—her security blanket. And until she was trained, she lived in an old bonus room at the bottom of the house—now Fred's office, now carpeted, with floor to ceiling bookshelves, a free-standing globe, an oversized desk made of pine; posters on the walls as well as a couple of framed black and white photos by Margaret Bourke-White (inherited); home to complicated communications systems, telephones and computers and fax machines. But back then it was empty and lined with linoleum. Fred would take her down at the end of the day and sing her to sleep. I'd hear him crooning from our bedroom on the floor above: "Something in the way she moves, attracts me like no other puppy . . ." and "There are puppies I remember . . ."

Upstairs by the fireplace stood a white stone pig with empty eyes that I'd found in a junk shop on La Cienega, and Roxy spent her evenings lying beside the staring, blind thing, absently licking its rough, no-color hooves. "She thinks it's her mother," my motherless husband would say. "She thinks no such thing. She doesn't know what it is, she doesn't recognize it by sight, it doesn't smell or feel like a mother to her. It's probably salty," I said. But I couldn't dissuade him.

"Most dogs are dogs," a friend once told me, "but Roxy is a duchess." Was it true? Was Roxy some kind of royalty in our midst? This dog who once shat all over the backseat of a car (never did get it completely cleaned up, attracted flies for two summers running, before we traded it in)? This dog—the one who quietly went through a wheel of brie on the General's coffee table, while ten of us ate our soup and salad on the other side of the room? The cur who systematically cleaned my kitchen floors with her tongue? Where's the dignity in any of that? But however singleminded and insatiable, noble she was: also a comfort—endlessly patient when we finally had a baby, and then another; when each of them jerked on her ears and her tail, and climbed over her back, and pulled her legs out from under her. Ever stoic—the dog with the soap in her eyes—I never heard her growl, not at them, not once. She'd get tired (those Labrador hips) and plop down in the middle of Go Fish or Monopoly, but she was, for the longest time, affable and game—up for a run or a chase, or to laze in the grass; to wait for the muse from under Fred's desk; to cheer me on from under the Steinway; and if one or the other of us retreated in anger or hurt, it wouldn't be long before we'd hear the clicking of her nails across the floors—the jingle of her tags on her collar—then feel the nudge of her nose behind a knee or in the crook of an elbow, evidence of her concern, her inclination to commiserate should we imagine ourselves lonely or alone. Eventually, of course, she started to gray around the muzzle—was less inclined, if we weren't evidently in distress, to follow us from room to room. Eventually, it got so she slept away most of the day; and as time went on, lame and creaky, riddled with lumps and bumps the way old dogs get, she began to seem not only tired but listless—not just resigned but down in the dumps; at which point we decided to find her some company.

This time, wisened up and politically correct, we didn't even think about *breeds*; we adopted an abandoned mutt with soft ears and big eyes, a beagle-dingo mix, with a red brindle coat. Fred named him Sullivan—Sully for short. The first few days were harder than we'd have predicted: there we were cavorting upstairs with our adorable pup, and the old girl wouldn't deign to join the party. Instead, she skulked down the spiral staircase and moped under the piano: *What betrayal was this?* she half groaned, half sighed. *How could we have done this to her?* she said with her eyes before she turned them to the wall. But towards the end of the week she came round, hobbled up the stairs one step at a time, one paw meeting the other like a crone with a cane, to check out the action. Within days, we were coming home to the two of them grooming each other like an old married couple. "Geez," Fred would say, "get a room." Peace then for a while—that is, after Sully went through two sets of Venetian Blinds and all the upholstery in the living room, Roxy, watching ruefully, no doubt, from the middle of the Kilim, her head between her paws. *You're gonna get it*, she'd have told him if she could. On the day that Sully went for sofa cushions—the feathers swirling and drifting out at us when we came home and opened the front door—Fred took out the vacuum, while I sat on the stoop and sobbed with Roxy's wet nose in my neck. Roxy. Solace. Solace. Roxy.

But she wasn't my dog, not really. She was Fred's all along. Would I have saved this collar? I don't know. And her ashes in a tin on a shelf in his office downstairs, wouldn't I have scattered them by now? Not up to me, thank goodness, collar and dog both just where they belong.

Meanwhile, Sully's grown old and white-faced, has lumps of his own, one runny eye, and a permanent growth, black and misshapen, under the other, from some old wound that never healed as it should have. And if Roxy broke us in, Fred and I—taught us how to worry, and love, and laugh, and grieve, it's Sully who raised up Eliza and Jake, who spends days in her room and nights in his. And it must be acknowledged: Roxy was unflappable, yes, but Sully is smart—multitalented in fact. He opens screen doors all by himself, and, if we neglect to take him to the park, hides our shoes in protest. He's as fast as any squirrel; can catch a ball on the fly; and Sully can sing. Gladly, he followed Eliza out to the decks to practice, back when she played the alto sax. With gusto, he howled along to "Take Five" for all the neighborhood to hear. However—of late he's less vocal, and also less spry; generally less engaged. A few weeks ago, because I decided he needed company—or maybe because I did (Eliza having left us for the other coast)—we adopted another mutt, a herder this time (she nips at our ankles, and takes Sully's leash in her mouth when we walk), partial to single socks, and given to squatting and peeing right in front of us like it's performance art. Skinny young thing, she kept slipping out of her collar (brown), until Fred, ever resourceful, poked through the leather with a lobster pick to make a new hole. She's an anxious creature, can't seem to settle; sniffs my heels as I write, half circles my chair, paces behind me, puts her snout in my lap. When I finally look up, she cocks her head as if to ask why we're sitting around: are we going to waste the whole day or what? I pick up Roxy's collar in both hands, and Elphie sniffs, grabs hold, and tugs; we face off then, I very stern, she duly admonished. Except she's not one to give in easily, no, and she cannot resist a tentative lick. Not that she knows it's a collar, or whose, or to pay proper respect. Nor does she think it's her mother, oh no.

It's me she looks to; and waits on; and loves.

CHARM

WHEN THE GRADUATE was born, her father gave me a pair of fine, old earrings—pearl drops from silver bows, Victorian, tiny gems strung along tarnished ribbons, just the vaguest hint of color there, a suggestion of sparkle, no more. I wore those earrings every day for a couple of years—but they dangled from French wires. And when the graduate was only a toddler, one of them up and evaporated. It was tax time, I remember—I'd had one in each ear when we left to see the accountant, but somewhere between the car and his office, maybe during a discussion about college savings, the pearl on the right side disappeared, never to be recovered. Devastating—but nothing to be done—I took the remaining trinket to a jeweler, who turned it into a charm to hang from a chain around my neck; but it was too lovely, too fragile a thing, meant for a person with a pronounced clavicle, a hollow at the base of her throat, a girl with delicate bones, like Eliza. The graduate.

Last week, along with some nine hundred other families, we snaked across Los Feliz Boulevard, crawled up Hillhurst and Vermont, found our way into a lot, stacked like everybody else, every space taken from below the Vermont Canyon tennis courts to way up above the Greek Theatre, where we filled the stadium, where we waited as every member of the Marshall High Class of 2008 was called one by one and in no particular order, to march in, collect a diploma, and then find a seat in the orchestra. Jake counted 917 names, but another friend was sure there were 921, and though, admittedly, I sniffled through the first five playbacks of "Pomp and Circumstance," by the forty-seventh, I was pretty much all cried out.

Then over to Chinatown with two other families for a celebratory lunch, sodas on the house for the three graduates, and when Jake, who will be a high school sophomore in the fall, asked for a Sprite, we told him he'd have to wait three years, take the requisite number of APs, visit the requisite number of colleges, fill out those applications, work a few more summers for his spending money, fight with us over chores, homework, car keys, what have you, before he collected on free soda. But all of that was tongue in cheek, since the truth is the graduate hasn't given us much trouble, focused as she's been on her future. (The future is its own reward in her case.) Eliza was determined from the beginning to attend college in the east, plans for junior year abroad, for graduate school, for life to finally begin on her terms three thousand miles away.

And never until now were we so aware of how short our tenure as parents, how brief this time together as a family. These roles—mother, father—so central to our definition of ourselves for the rest of our lives, this radiant young woman so central to our imaginations, waking and sleeping: "Don't make me cry, Mom," she says, and it's because she says it, that I know I'm allowed to weep if I want.

But what's to cry about? She was a pole vaulter in high school, remember? Assuming we've done this right, all of us, she's supposed to catapult herself up, over, and into a life that hopefully will include us in some peripheral way. It's not that she won't be back—but while she will remain at the center of our lives, other people, other relationships, will take on paramount importance in her own. That's as it should be, we tell ourselves, that's how it's done.

Just before lunch at Yang Chow, we give Eliza the charm wrapped in tissue and ribbon. It's pretty enough, but small and old-fashioned—not something she'd have chosen for herself, I don't suppose. And yet it's perfect; its original significance underscored and amplified by occasion times two. We know this, we three, connected as we are in this moment and the one that came before. After she's unwrapped it and thanked us—and fastened it around her neck—she remembers to open her card: on the front, a girl reading in a chair which is hovering above the grass, as if having achieved liftoff and about to careen into space. *Be safe,* I wanted to write on the inside—and *buckle up,* and *hold on,* and a dozen other cautionary aphorisms.

But Fred had a better idea: "How about *Enjoy the ride?*"

FLIGHT JACKET

INGRATE. MY DAUGHTER the beautiful ingrate. It was supposed to have gone with her to college, to Boston. That was the plan, and she left it in her closet. Look here, my flight jacket, with the green ticket stub from the dry cleaner safety-pinned to one of the knit cuffs, which are brown and stretchy and ribbed, as is the waistband; guess I didn't know any better when I was twenty-one, didn't know I only wanted leather, all leather, nothing stretchy, nothing smacking of counterfeit. It was a find, a treasure, twenty bucks for a flight jacket in a narrow, basement shop on Seventy-Seventh Street in 1978. Now I'd sniff—now I'd second-guess; now I haven't the conviction to buy what I want, don't even know what I want, can't seem to choose, no joy in shopping anymore—but back then, oh my, I almost trusted myself. Now I'd turn up my nose at nylon or Banlon, or whatever it is; plus it *doesn't* have one of those fake fur collars. Still. It has epaulets with snaps. More snaps on the flaps of the front pockets, and at the top and the bottom of the brass zipper, which has twice been replaced. Inside, the lining, a silk the color of a muddy cup of coffee, is frayed beyond salvation across the back of the neckline. The ancient label inside the collar says *Fine Leather Wear*, the L in red script and nearly invisible. Below that in block letters: Made in U.S.A.

My old flight jacket. So shabby I've had to stop wearing it; unbecoming for a woman of my age and station—a person who shows up to back-to-school nights and college information sessions—can't walk around in a jacket rubbed to raw, the sort of item another person might pull out of Dumpster and keep in her shopping cart under the trestle at Sunset and Alvarado: Can't wear it to work; can't wear it out to dinner; can't wear it to a black tie event with a little black dress—I'm just too old—can't even wear it with jeans worn at the knees, which I also shouldn't be wearing, don't think I don't worry about that, too. But imagine: I only figured out that my jacket was unrespectable—inappropriate—about a year ago. Up until then it didn't occur to me I needed something to cover my ass, something slightly more dignified. At which point I put my old friend in the back of the car to take to Goodwill. Except I couldn't part with it. Except Goodwill wouldn't have had it if I could. I brought it back to the house, laid it over the banister to be taken downstairs and hung in the dark of my closet.

But then. Eliza mosied down one day to ask where my leather jacket was and if it could be repaired. She pulled it out and modeled for me: my gorgeous girl, who puts no premium on vintage, on cashmere darned at the elbows, on already-been-used—most especially on anything already used by me. And yet she wanted my jacket! It was *cool*, she said. Back into the car with me—with it—and over to the cleaners, where an Asian woman, herself partial to sequined sweaters, politely threw up her hands; couldn't do a thing for it, she said, except to stitch it back together where the sleeves had come apart at the seams; and that for twice what the jacket had cost me a quarter century prior. I called Eliza from the counter to ask what she thought: it wouldn't keep her warm or dry, after all, worn at the elbows to the thickness of a quality paper napkin. But she claimed she wanted it even so—and I was delighted; picked it up a few days later, all in one piece at least, draped in cellophane on a double wire hanger. And here it is. She left it home.

Thirty years ago, just out of college, I bought this jacket in that tiny junk shop, which means it was already soaked in secrets, reeking of the past. I lived on Second Avenue in a sixth-floor walk-up. Waited tables at a comedy club on First, and dawdled my way down the two long avenue blocks to work, squandered my afternoons in the side-street storefronts, where I picked up old linens, handkerchiefs, mismatched glassware, costume jewelry, and ancient sheet music that might or might not serve as audition material (I was always on the lookout for sixteen bars that nobody had ever heard before). June was hot, and July was hotter, and August was the worst—nearly didn't make it through August—didn't know who I was or who I wanted to be, didn't know how to live alone, how to feed myself, how to get through the long days till the night shift. Then came September and the smell of autumn, and even though, for the first time in memory, I wasn't going back to school, I took comfort when the wind picked up and the temperature dropped. Must have been then, in September, that I found the jacket, in excellent condition, and just the thing to get me through the winter months, along with a white silk scarf (a single tea stain on the under side), and a black felt fedora.

And this I remember: I'd only had it for a week or so when my parents arranged to take me to dinner at the Cookery downtown, to catch Alberta Hunter, whom I wanted them to hear, whom I'd heard myself a half a dozen times, though I couldn't afford it, though I had no business paying the cover, much less the minimum; I, with nothing in my fridge but a box of Wheat Thins, a six pack of Miller, and a jar of Grey Poupon. A blustery evening, and I put on my new old flight jacket and caught the subway at Seventh-Seventh and Lexington all the way down to Fourteenth Street, arriving at the restaurant somehow elated and unreasonably proud: That I knew my way around? That I had a job, an apartment, and a great, big dream? That I'd found myself a leather jacket, better than new, for twenty dollars even, no tax because I'd paid cash? My stepfather couldn't get enough of my goings-on, whereas my mother was mildly irritated to think I was on a first name basis with the maître d'. I, hardly able to make my rent, a regular in a nightclub. "A person of your means, Dinah," she murmured in disapproval, as he showed us to our ringside table.

We ordered, what? My favorites? Shrimp cocktail? Skinny fries? Stuffed mushrooms? My parents were buying—as they've done so many

times before and since—and I sat between them, a celebrity for the evening, in spite of my otherwise dubious status in the world. I must have
been desperately lonely, though I wouldn't have said that was what ailed
me at the time; but I remember now, as if I were eavesdropping—a
stranger watching from a table in the corner—that I talked from the moment I sat down and right through the New York cheesecake; first, about
my new purchase, which they'd admired right away; then, undoubtedly,
about my job in the club; maybe about the smells and sounds that wafted
up six flights from Second Avenue, about auditions at the Ansonia Hotel
and how I might want to do summer stock, about wanting to go to acting school; and yes, I was making my rent, and no, I wasn't working too
hard, I'd get by. And then—much too soon in all likelihood, since I was
on a wonderful roll, such a relief to talk and talk—out came Alberta, well
into her eighties, greeting me as if we were friends, blowing me a kiss
with a bejeweled, brown hand. She started her set, strutted and swayed
in place, one foot tapping, fingers snapping just off the beat—and when
she turned her head to wink at us now and then, her old earlobes were so
long and so heavy, they followed behind her.

It's only now—because I have a son who brims with news, revelations,
observations, ebullience—that I have a real sense of the way my parents
listened that evening; the way they've listened so many times before and
since. I didn't know what to do with all that *stuff* back then—to be an actor is to wait for permission to pour your intensity into a role, and the
opportunities are few and far between. I didn't understand that I had the
wherewithal to buff the daily to a high sheen all by myself. My impulse
was to take to the stage, to shout to anyone who would listen; to throw
up every thought as if it would catch momentum, take on a life of its
own, spin out into some pattern that signified. Signified, what? Meaning, import—inevitability, I guess. I must have supposed that if I talked
loud enough—if I *projected*—my path would be revealed. Truth is, all
those words flung every which way—they mostly evaporated. More like
soap bubbles than balls, or plates, or whirling batons. Meanwhile, I only
pretend I know what we talked about that night—what *I* talked about—in
truth I don't really remember. How can I? It's not like I wrote it down.

But one moment stays absolutely true and clear, as if it had only just happened: Was it towards the end of the set? Was it the encore, perhaps? I want to say it was. Alberta stopped swaying, stood perfectly still at the mike, and sang "The Glory of Love." And when she got to the bridge, Ron reached across the table, over my plate and glass, without looking at me, and took my mother's hand.

In that instant, I felt silly and extraneous and young; as aware of my parents as they were suddenly oblivious to me; two people in the middle of a sustained and exclusive conversation—I just happened to be there, just happened to get a glimpse and a glimmer of a panorama that I couldn't have understood fully, not at the time. Isn't it funny, if not for that one moment—between *them*—I'm sure I wouldn't remember the rest of the evening at all. The beginning of my life—and the life of a second-hand flight jacket—underscored for all time with a single image that had nothing whatsoever to do with me.

GREEN EARRINGS

I WATCHED MY mother dress when she let me. When she was in the mood. She was like the woman in the Alka Seltzer commercial all those years ago, remember? Her reflection in the mirror, hair piled and pinned on top of her head, tracing her eyes with a pointed black brush, powdering and sponging, pulling the mascara wand up through her lashes, lips last thing—but did she line them? Did she color them in? (I had a teacher like that in second grade, Mrs. Averback, outlined her lips in dark red, then filled them in with something pale and frosted. She must have looked like a clown, but we didn't think so, we called her ravishing.) Finishing touches applied, the actress came to life. But it was the spell of those preparations—that methodical seduction—that reminded me: to witness firsthand, close up—my mother, I mean—the thrill, the thrall of watching her from my perch on the lid of the toilet seat, she moving about me in various states of undress, in and out of the tub, the bathroom fragrant with Secret of Venus. Sometimes I was allowed to pour from the bottle, heavy and rectangular, held between my palms and carefully angled just so, to release a few intoxicating drops; then she swished the amber oil around with her fingers, and I chattered and she mused, and her breasts floated up like enormous lotuses, nipples peeking through the steam, and her face got pink, and she pushed her wet hair back behind her ears. Afterward—did she make up first, or did she dress? Either way, I was her company while she shadowed her eyes in gray, as she fastened her bra, pulled on sheer hose—then slipped into velvet, or silk, or cashmere, or wool, pinned a brooch at her neckline, bracelets at her wrists, rings on her fingers. Later, scarved against the cold, something wrapped in tissue and ribbon in her gloved hands—a hostess gift—she stood at the door, with Ron, my stepfather, in suit and tie. And as she turned to leave, it flashed: a pale, round star in the lobe of her ear; a circle of a stone shot through with light—not emerald, or chartreuse, or aquamarine—a color like no other, faceted, rimmed in black enamel and gold and studded with tiny diamonds.

I would have been around twelve when Leah first bought the earrings from a jeweler in Jerusalem. "You will have them," she'd promise each time she took them from their pouch. "They will be yours when you're thirty-five." Thirty-five. My god, who would ever be thirty-five. (She, herself, wasn't yet thirty-five.) Content to wait, I borrowed the earrings from time to time straight through my twenties: my mother always generous that way, with this cameo, that locket, this bracelet, those rings. She'd open the safe in the cabinet under the bathroom sink; we'd sit cross-legged on the cold tile, she, and I, and my sister, and my mother would help us pick for the occasion, whatever it was (a party, a prom); each heirloom mounted in the finest gold, nothing plated, nothing that wasn't one of a kind: the coral drops? The amethysts? Not the diamonds, no (too old, too grand for either of us), and not the pearls, too prissy (for me anyway)—we chose with some combination of delight and awe, decorated ourselves, and off we went to wherever we were going as if we owned the stuff, as if it were ours.

By the time I turned thirty-five, I lived in Los Angeles. I had a little girl of my own. My mother came to visit around the time of my birthday and, all business, took me to Armani on Rodeo Drive, where she bought

me a bottle green suit—skirt, wide-legged trousers, and a jacket with a
narrow lapel. My knees shook just slightly as I shuffled a pirouette on
a low stool for the in-house seamstress, who, for her part, was able to
crouch in high heels and a pencil skirt without toppling over, in order
to take up the hem of my fancy new trousers. Not once that day—nor
for the remainder of her stay—did either of us, my mother or I, mention
the earrings. It was the following year, I think, or maybe the year after,
when she sat me down in front of a square velvet box, grim-faced, and
ordered me to open it. Inside, a pair of earrings, rimmed in black and
gold and diamonds, but the stone was jade—solid, dull, without mystery.
Impressive to be sure, an otherwise perfect replica of the earrings from
another planet. I must have gasped, or startled, or bit my lip. I must have
murmured something—but what? *Wow. Gee. How did you manage . . . ?* I
only remember my mother's mouth tightened then—that she searched
my face for a moment before her own features closed down. I put the
open box back on the table in front of me. Placed my hands in my lap.
"Amazing." I said. "Yes," she agreed, "They are." And she mentioned, not
looking at me, that she'd gone to considerable expense. "Be honest now,"
she said. "Which would you prefer? The copies, or the originals?" And
this part I can't forget:
    "You want me to be honest?"
    "Yes."
    "Well, then, the originals. The originals, of course."
    It was my mother who closed the box. Stood up, hands trembling, her
anger rising like a sudden stench, vaporous and overwhelming. "And you
will never have them," she said. She turned and left the room.

From her point of view this would be a tale of ingratitude. And how to
convince her otherwise? I didn't want her earrings—I didn't have to have
them, not ever, certainly not on a schedule. The promise was enough;
enough for me to be the heir apparent. I was, perhaps, more comfortable
than I should have been in that role, whereas, my mother carried the
burden of my expectation as if I were her peer instead of her daughter—
as if there weren't a generation between us (just barely); she, in her fif-

ties, after all, was a woman at the *other* end of middle age—consequently aware, in a way I wasn't, not yet, of the passing of time. It was the finality of her decision that slayed me that day. The promise not broken, but altogether revoked; the determination to punish me for what she understood as my sense of entitlement. As if I weren't willing to wait. As if I'd have been grateful either way. And as if I'd have ever backed down from what we both knew—that the one pair of stones was infinitely more dazzling than the other. Was it her prerogative to hang on to her stuff (her beauty, her youth) for as long as she liked? It was. But was it my obligation to pretend? To indulge her, as if one or the other of us didn't know any better? But it was she who'd cultivated my taste and sensibility in the first place. Long and short, we barely spoke for the rest of her visit. I pushed the velvet box to the back of my sock drawer.

A few years went by, and my mother lost and found one of the earrings, not once but twice. The second time, when the missing stud turned up in a hotel room long after she'd returned home, she handed the pair over to me and took back the copies for herself. "A sign," she said, as if she believed in such things. "Are you sure?" I asked. "It's time," she said. And that was all.

I'm thinking again about the woman in the commercial: After the lips, blotted with a tissue, was it then that she pulled the pin from her hair, black as my mother's, and let it cascade around her shoulders? Or did she put the tablets in the glass first? Of course she did! *Plop, plop, fizz, fizz*—so went the jingle—and *then* the hair came tumbling down . . . That woman was magnificent to me in the way of my magnificent mother, until, that is, she shook out her hair and smiled at herself in the mirror. Leah's hair never tumbled: it was wound in a French twist at the back of her head; then all cut off—think Jean Seberg or Audrey Hepburn—sometime in her thirties. My mother, always in her thirties in my mind—is that when I first began to contemplate the ways in which we were not the same? First saw myself as separate? Coming up short in some departments, and not in others: I was suddenly taller than she and not so voluptuous; there were things she was interested in that I wasn't; and things, it turned out, I could do that she could not. And yet. Aware as I imagined I was of our perimeters defined, around that time I began to wear my hair in a twist, to borrow her finery, to want and wait to become, in her eyes more than anyone's, somebody almost exactly like her.

We continue to live on different sides of the continent now, my mother and I; don't see each other enough, and when we do, I'm as vaguely surprised to discover she is old, as she must be to discover I am older. But if she's forever thirty-five in my mind's eye, does that mean I'm presenting somehow as a fifteen-year-old girl? Certainly not. My mother, myself. I'm permanently thirty-five, too.

What's more, as she did, I cut off the hair—have worn it short for over a decade. It's still mostly dark, and my bones are strong; and my mother's jewels—though I wear them seldom (my lifestyle doesn't support them)— still become me on the right occasions. But I'm over fifty now, with a daughter in college, a daughter becoming more herself every day—not that she has ever been tempted to confuse her persona with mine. Odd to think, though, assuming my theory holds, that Eliza will remember me best as I am right now: almost as old as my mother was when she finally surrendered the earrings.

A decade ago, and a few years after she gave them up, Leah one day appraised my profile from the passenger seat of my car. "You have about five good years left," she said with eerie objectivity. At the time, turning to meet her gaze—those lips, those eyes!—I tamped down a shudder and nodded to match her affect, to mask my hurt and fear (*was it true?*), resolved to pass what felt like a test (*of course it was—so said my mother*). I would not be shallow, I would not be vain. I would be as clinical as she, as if we were talking about somebody else, as if I'd known all along, had already considered, in fact, and come to the same conclusion. In truth, her prescience, not her dispassion, took my breath. It didn't occur to me in the moment that my mother, herself well past my projected sell-by date, was anything but deeply wise. And beautiful, too.

More recently I wore the green earrings with the bottle green suit to some sort of luncheon. Met a friend afterwards for coffee. "Oh Dinah," she gasped, facing me across the table. "You've lost an earring—." I touched my fingers to both lobes, went red in the face, started to sweat and swear. But by some kind of miracle, retracing our steps, traipsing up and down the block eyes to the ground, we found the missing gem in the gutter within the hour. Someone had stepped on it, flattened the wire and cracked the stone, but somehow the whole had survived in its setting. It's since been repaired; you'd have to look hard to see any difference between the two. But did I take the episode as some kind of sign? My turn to pass the earrings on, perhaps? I didn't, no. Had I thought about it, I'd have been more likely to return them to their original owner, but instead I somehow convinced myself they were really and truly mine. No doubt they will go to my daughter someday—although for now anyway she isn't the least bit interested in my belongings. She wears her sun-streaked hair as she pleases, and is partial to silver. Not gold.

LITTLE BLACK DRESS

SHOULD YOU PACK the dress? The little black dress? A sleeveless shift, darts at the bust, comes to just above the knee, meant to be worn with hose and heels, black on black, diamonds at the wrist, jewels dripping from the ears, lips lined in red, eyes lined in charcoal and heavily mascara-ed, the wand pulled through each lash real slow at the corners, the way you've been taught.

This dress—this is the dress that got you through—through and past and over the Opening, the Wrap, the Gala; that Christmas, that New Year's, that Black Tie event; a parade of your own anniversaries and birthdays, and everybody else's big one, besides. For this dress you bought a succession of pointy-toed pumps, pashminas, and push-up bras; it's this dress that gave the old Ford its cool (and the Dodge, and the mini-van too in their day), that allowed you to descend from the passenger seat with a modicum of moxie, to give the Beast (you called it the Beast, big as it was, its ceiling rigged with popsicle sticks when it started to fall) to the valet at the Beverly Hills Hotel, the Bel Air, the Four Seasons, and even outside that gated monstrosity in Hancock Park, the pink stucco affair with the gargoyles on either side of the wrought iron gates across the driveway.

How many times in this dress, have you swung your legs—swathed in sheer Lycra with a seam up the back—around like a diver, to step from the car, to rise to almost six feet, to tower over the guy in the bow tie and vest in your three inch heels, to look down at him, all demure, all murmured thanks, when he called you "Miss"; as if you looked like a Miss, and as if you were driving a shiny new Jag—you wish—but you didn't look like you wished, not then, not yet.

Oh, you should be able to say when you bought this dress and what for . . . But you don't remember . . . That's the problem; the dress is that old—the seams beginning to loosen and disappear under the arms, the color fading there, too. Should you pack the dress? Should you ever wear the little black dress again? Should you?

You should buy a new dress, that's what you should do. And you've been dutifully folding down the corners in your catalogues, surfing the net, dropping over to Nordstrom's on weekday mornings, when the dressing rooms are empty, trying on dress after dress in three-way mirrors, under unforgiving fluorescent lights. Except. Except, this one has capped sleeves (unacceptable) and that one, an empire waist (flattering to whom?); not a garment can you find without lace at the hem (precious), a bow at the shoulder (puerile), gratuitous puckers, pleats, and pockets; all you want is a little black dress like the one you already have. Except, except . . .

When did it happen? When—how—did the lipstick get too dark, the eyeliner too severe? When, by the way, did people start telling you to color your hair? And when oh when did every occasion in the little black dress begin to feel just a little like Halloween?

So. Is it actually, finally time to retire the little black dress? You sit on the edge of the bed, the dress spread across your lap.

You remember a dinner party in Laurel Canyon. Back in the days when you needed a sitter. (That baby nearly grown now, has her own black dress, left it in the back of the closet when she went away to school; she didn't need it.) A party in a house on stilts; a woman there—a guest like you—petite and pale, boneless, with eczema on the fleshy backs of her arms, and yellow teeth, and halitosis. Somehow even so, she commandeered the evening, excluded you, it seemed, from every conversation, gazed at something just over your shoulder when you did speak, though she cultivated a special intimacy with everyone else at the table, even your husband, whom, you remember (how can you forget?) she invited to play poker the following week. Small and rubbery as she was, she slithered up close to him; to everyone but you, men and women alike—if they'd had awnings growing out of their eyebrows, she'd have been in the shade. You wondered, from exile, how they didn't back away from her, since you could smell her breath from where you were, though she said nothing directly to you all evening, not a word. Except. Except, "That's quite a dress," she hissed, not meeting your eye, as you passed each other in the hall, coming and going from the bathroom. You thanked her—you thanked her retreating back, that is—and she vaguely waved from over her shoulder.

You smooth the dress across your knees. You snap a thread hanging from the hem. Flick away a bit of lint near the neckline. You fold it in half lengthwise, lay it across the top of the suitcase, just so. You'll wear trousers, no doubt, with a silk and cashmere blend button-down cardigan, very appropriate. But—just in case—you're packing the little black dress.

LITTLE BLACK DRESS, TWO

I DIDN'T WANT the gig.

The best new show on television, sure, but I was holding out for a real part, a solid guest star. I wanted, for instance, to die (conscious to the end) in a bed; or I wanted to watch (visibly and audibly distraught) while somebody else died in a bed. I wanted a role with heft, range, arc. I'd been a regular on a series—granted, it was canceled after six episodes—but, I'd proved my mettle. I was deserving. Except actors, come to find out, aren't even as good as their last jobs, besides which a couple of pregnancies had taken me out of circulation.

Even so. *I'll wait for something bigger,* I told my manager (I had a manager then) and she told the casting director, and he told her to tell me not to be an ass, the role could recur. Three lines—it didn't seem worth it—but my manager reminded me, it wasn't like the offers were pouring in. I'd been auditioning for Woman Jurist, Woman Reporter, Woman in Sales, and, worst of all, just plain *Woman.* Meanwhile, here was a real scene with one of the stars of the show, and the lines, though there were only three, had some umph. Plus, I had a name this time: not *Woman,* but *Shirley,* Nurse Shirley to you.

I took the part. I got to the set. I was swathed in blue from head to toe, masked, hatted, gowned, gloved, goggled—unrecognizable except for my voice (*Dinah, I heard you last night on TV*); maybe I did two episodes that first season; none at all the second. But then, the third, suddenly they were regularly writing me into the show; and, after that, if they didn't, I'd send letters to ask if I'd retired, or was I only on sabbatical, in which case, I pleaded, bring me back, please bring me back, in pink or green (blue is for surgery), give me a last name and move me to the ER where the nurses bare their faces more often than not.

Nothing doing, Shirley, said the writers. *Once a surgical nurse, always a surgical nurse.*

Still, each time I thought it was over, the call would come in: eighty-something shows in fifteen years, and occasionally, I'd even have something fun to play. Mysterious though she was, there were clues to Shirley: she collected Buddy Holly records; she was married; she was prickly and irreverent and bossy; and her all-time favorite surgeon was Dr. Morgenstern, William H. Macy, that is—what good taste she had.

Shirley pushed the plot (and the gurneys) at worst; at best she was comic relief, but either way I took her seriously. One time—we were shooting the one hundredth episode—I entered on cue and said my single line to Dr. Benton (played by a guy who'd been on the cover of *TV Guide*), informing him with the *teeniest* bit of attitude that he had people waiting for him in his office.

CUT! roared the director, a theatrical presence with a strong mid-Atlantic lilt.

Out he came into the hall to whisper in my ear: "I think that was a bit judgmental, don't you?"

Yes, it was judgmental! I was acting! The scene was all about me, you didn't get that?

"Know your lines and don't bump into the furniture," advised Spencer Tracy. But how to spend eight to ten hours on a set and not do what I'd been trained to do? It took me years to learn to tone it down: for years, no kidding, I worked these brows, reacted to every line whether or not I was on camera, believed and wished and hoped, until I didn't anymore; until I realized I wouldn't be *discovered* on *ER*. After that I kept my fingers crossed—no close-ups, please—if my words were covered in a two shot or even the master, I might get home in time for supper.

Periodically, the mask would actually come off, or I'd get eight lines instead of five. I'd joke then about *Tootsie*, the movie—how one of these days I'd take the scalpel into my own hands. One time a series regular saw through my act: "You know it won't happen," she said. "You achieve a certain status on this show, and that's where you stay." In her tenure (not as long as my own), she'd gone from guest starring, to starring, to eventually directing. So how did she know about me? About Shirley? How did she know what I'd only pretended to accept? And what did she care if I deluded myself? My exuberance—my innate optimism—must have annoyed her to the point that she felt compelled to tell me: know your lines, don't bump into the furniture, get on with your life.

And so I did. I played my other roles: wife, mother, daughter, teacher, friend. Not that I ever took Shirley for granted, because I couldn't, I didn't have a contract. But I stopped longing for a last name and a plot line of my own. Although busy as I was with family, friends, career, I never stopped hoping for one more episode. Because it was a gig, not because I was invested. Or so I thought.

The night of the final wrap I was in decent spirits, having managed to shimmy into my little black dress (not yet retired)—which, I realized as I pulled it up over my hips, I'd almost certainly bought for my first *ER* gala a dozen years before. And unabashedly worn to a half a dozen celebrations of the show, with mostly the same cast and crew in attendance each time. On this night, true to form, Fred admired me as if the dress were new, as if it and I (and I in it) were admiration-worthy. Off we went to the party, staged in a sprawling Hollywood Club, where, when we arrived, there were already hundreds of people, and dozens of TVs in all corners of every room; multiple episodes airing all at the same time. While Fred filled a plate at the buffet, then found two chairs at a table full of strangers, I stood at the bar—ornately carved from ice and consequently dripping all over my pointy black shoes—and waited for a glass of wine. I scanned the room: waved at this one, grinned at that—but easy enough to avoid the shmooze, and so began my unraveling; how strange that I didn't know any of these people any better than I'd known them at the start.

There were speeches, of course, and a long reel of moments to remember: cast photos, finally, with a cake as big as a California King. These parties had never been fun, not exactly, but somewhere in the middle of posing (way over to the right, last row) it hit me—this was the last one I'd ever endure—the very last time I'd wonder if I should step up for the cameras with the rest; if I should take pains to shake the executive producer's hand; if I should bother to find the writers who'd regularly given me work; if anybody had noticed I was wearing the little black dress all over again; if any of the rigmarole would inform my future in any way. I was suddenly undone—sad and sorry it was over—having mostly to do, I was afraid, with how little it finally meant to me; and what did *that* say about who I am, who I'd wanted to be, and how it had all turned out?

I held it together till we got in the car, and then I cried all the way home. Where I took off my old dress, stepped into pajamas, and got ready for bed. Who was I kidding to think I wasn't sentimentally attached? For though my real life had unfurled worlds away from Stage 3 on the Warner Brothers lot, and though I seemed to have taken not a single real relationship with me, at long last I'd lost Shirley. Shirley, whom I hardly knew at all. Whom I knew, on the other hand, almost as well as I know myself.

FERRIS WHEEL

I CAN ALMOST promise—almost—I'll never skydive, not me.

It's not that I haven't considered it. Standing out on the deck, I can call up the feeling. Have I dreamed it? I think I have: myself suspended in the sky above Kite Hill towards the end of the day—Mount Baldy to the east, snowcapped, and in the other direction the sun bouncing off the skyscrapers downtown as if to set them on fire. I can even imagine jumping, pulling the cord, the silk ballooning out behind me, first drawing me up before I start to drift down like a spider, arms and legs spread wide. See, I've read, I've heard—I even know people, several, in fact, who, on the eve of a big birthday or anniversary, wrote checks for a few hundred bucks apiece, and leapt into the sky.

My feeling? Flying is for birds—unless your feathers plume and fan; unless you're able to glide on the span of your wings; or they move so fast (tiny as they are) that you can tread air with your beak in the blooms, flying is unnatural, and only at its *most* unnatural—in an oversized bus with wings—is it acceptable to me. Or rather, only then can I suspend my disbelief, having to do with my agenda, which is to get from here to there. In which case, the fact of flying is incidental; certainly, it isn't something you'd do for its own sake; it is rather, something you've done as long as you can remember: you—that is I, whose parents lived in different states from the time I was in first grade; so I therefore shuttled back and forth in a frock and Mary Janes, since (back then) flying—or landing at any rate—was an event worth dressing for. But even then, especially then, I didn't quite get it; I simply did as I was told, less concerned about how I got from Logan to La Guardia, than about who would be waiting for me in either place.

And so it is now: each time, at the airport, I board as if bored. Each time, in flight, glancing out and down, I might be reminded: *I'm in a plane! Look! There's the ocean—I could pluck up that sailboat and stow it in my pocket; I could wipe the foam off the shore with my pinky; I could swallow that cloud.* At which point, mind sufficiently boggled, I'll lean back and close my eyes. Or open my book.

Chicken that I am (if I'm any kind of bird), I'm not about to actually test my nerve, nor do I feel in need of a mid-life reckoning, no—not the dangerous kind, not from any great height. But if I were told that I couldn't? That I wouldn't have the chance, not ever again? What am I afraid of, really? How likely am I to expire because I didn't open my parachute? Not likely—not at all—so it's not dying, it's living that scares me: not climbing, swimming, paddling, not moving up or towards—I can do all those things. It's standing on the edge—it's just before the jump. It's fear of dangling, that's what it is.

Oh where is my courage? And—and what is courage anyway? Is it the same thing as fearlessness? No. No, it seems to me if a person is fearless, she doesn't need courage. Courage is for those of us who are actually scared. Courage is a choice. Unless there isn't one, in which case we must be brave, mustn't we?

Till we are. Say, maybe you think it comes easy to me, but you can't imagine—because you haven't stood in the wings—the sensation as the house lights go down and the overture begins. You haven't felt your heart pound, and your throat close up, the lyrics gone from your head moments before you're to enter the scene for the very first time. What was it all those opening nights that propelled me out onto the stage, courage or fear? Sometimes a person finds herself at the edge, that's all. She has to act.

When the kids were small, when I would have done about anything to break up a Sunday afternoon, I once took them down to some sort of festival in Echo Park, where there wasn't a Ferris wheel the day before, and there wouldn't be one the next; but presto, there it was, and they wanted a ride. I bought three yellow tickets, then seated myself between them holding tight to their hands. Back we swung back with a jolt, and then forward and up: no belts, no latches, no straps of any kind—just a metal bar in front of us—lucky for me, they were (they are) good children, and sensible, and fundamentally kind; not about to let go, not about to lean too far over the side, even then as concerned for me as I was for them— and even so, I rued the decision. *Anyway,* I thought, *this will be over soon and we will be fine.*

Up, up we went, till we saw the tops of the oaks, the palms, the old magnolias—below us, the lotuses blooming velvety against the black of the lake—though, I admit, I only saw all that from the corner of my eye, afraid as I was to be distracted from my task, which was to focus straight ahead as if we weren't climbing higher and higher (too high), swinging precariously this way and that; as if my stomach hadn't dropped, as if I weren't breathing hard, a sour taste on the back of my tongue. My job howbeit to will us around and down again, onto our feet, on which we'd walk, like sensible bi-peds, to the boathouse to rent something small with paddles or oars, which I'd navigate all by myself, thanks, between and among the swans.

But then—then in the middle of this act of will something went wrong—the Ferris wheel stopped at the highest point, and we *dangled* there, for minutes—for many minutes—and I considered this contraption, which would be in pieces and packed into the back of a truck by nightfall; wondered how sturdy it might not be—looked up at the carriage swaying, creaking in its joint as if it might snap, and, I thought, *Well, if we must die, we will die together. Poor Fred,* I thought. (I told him so later.) "Ssshhhhh," I said to the children, who hadn't uttered a word, both of them beaming, thrilled to be above the trees.

There's no height Eliza won't scale, no terrain she won't travel, very few things she's unwilling to try. Since high school, one way or another I've been watching from the bleachers, which is when and where I maybe first understood (though I've had to be reminded again and again) how different she is from me. I'd hold onto my elbows not breathing as she ran toward the sand pit, placed the pole, sailed up and over the bar—or not. Who'd want to do such a thing? Who'd risk that jump and for what? A few moments in the air? To say she did? To be *herself.*

We had three days to get her settled in Boston: to find winter boots and a rug for her dorm room—neither of which we found—though we did stumble into a Bed Bath & Beyond, where armed with back-to-school savings coupons, we purchased hangers, soap, throw pillows, a shower caddy, and one of those clip-on lamps. We don't usually run out of things to talk about, Eliza and I, but that weekend was tough. We both knew what was coming. Was she afraid? She must have been, in her way. But we were on the wheel, no getting off, no turning back. *Look straight ahead,* I told myself, *and you'll both be fine.*

On the last day, after the Convocation Ceremony, we went back to her room.

I sat on her bed. "I guess I better go," I said.

"Not yet," she said.

"What shall we do then?"

She looked at the floor. "I guess you better go."

I gathered my things—she put her new key in her pocket—and we walked down a couple of flights, out through heavy metal doors and into late afternoon sunshine. Oh the ache behind my eyes and at the back of my throat. Though the rental car was only around the corner, a short block away, we agreed—no discussion—to say goodbye on the sidewalk just outside the building.

"Promise not to look back, okay, Mom?"

"Okay," I said. Talk about vertigo.

"I mean it, Mom."

"Okay."

She broke from me then, and I lurched forward—took three steps and swayed; and then, how not, turned to see my beauty skimming the sidewalk—running, sailing, flying, as prescribed, straight into her life. So what to do next, dangle there? Why, no. No choice at all, but to turn, face forward, and hang on for the rest of the ride.

STICK KITE

SAY, LITTLE GIRL — I dream of you. You then, you now. You, as you are, coming into my room to ask if you can go through my closet, rummage in my drawers and jewelry boxes; might you borrow that sweater, can you have this ring, and the copy of *Anna Karenina* over there on the shelf, you want that, too—and, by the way, you ask on your way out with the sweater and the ring (not the book, you can't have the book), *is that me or you in the photo there?* I look up from whatever I'm doing: *Which photo do you mean?* That one, 10" x 14", framed on the wall, sepia-toned: the one of the exquisite child in the wide-brimmed hat—big eyes looking up at the camera—her face lit from below by the flashlight in her hands: *Is it you or is it me*, you ask again. Why, it's you, darling! Of course it is. You thought so, you say. You were confused—having to do with the snapshot upstairs—the faded three by five black-and-white in the bookshelves; and yes, you're right—that is I, no question—I'm the kid with the gap-toothed grin and crooked bangs sticking out from under the cowboy hat: though how do I know? It's not as if I remember wearing it.

But this likeness? *This* little girl? I *animate* this moment—and her: you, that is—you in your life, taking on the camera, looking straight into the lens. You don't remember?—how you dressed as a witch, though you'd planned to be a cat (abandoned whiskers at the last minute for a sheet; the sheet then abandoned for conical headgear); maybe now, now that I've told you, you recall something of the night; the shrieks and whoops, the jack-o-lantern whose nose you designed with a sharpee for me to carve; maybe you remember peering into a strange living-room from somebody's stoop while I waited on the sidewalk. I bet you do. But I remember the flash of the bulb—and the street we were on; the laughter out of nowhere, the rustle of the wind in the trees, and kids running, swirling this way and that as if blown with the leaves. The last night of October, and the air in Los Angeles suddenly nippy; I can hear you re-fusing to put on a sweater, face flushed, warm fingers wrapped around mine—*I'm not cold*, you said. And afterwards: how you sat on the floor with an old pillowcase full of candy, and how we bartered, you and I; how you couldn't be bribed or dissuaded from keeping the Kit Kats and the plain M&M's—but you would remember which varieties you liked best, whereas I remember *you*. I know the feel of your arms around my neck, the smell of chocolate on your breath. I'm the one who can tell you how it was, how you were. Just ask. Ask about the first time you laughed; how you looked when you didn't want to cry; how long it took you to fall asleep: it's I who remembers the sound of you singing to yourself when you didn't know I was listening, and I can summon your tiny person, running far out on the flats at low tide on Thumpertown Beach, with a wand in your hand, a stick kite, the streamers—bright blue, yellow, or-ange, green—flying out behind you. Do you remember that day? Cloud-less? You shading your eyes as you ran? And that toy: those long silky ribbons like the sail to your skiff? Maybe you do. But that moment—that moment in your life—I claim that one, too; as if it belonged to me.

III.

SCOOP

PEOPLE ARE SO fundamentally hopeful, aren't they, and all the time looking for *signs*. You meet the one, and the fact that your parents, both sets, drank Chock full o'Nuts strikes you as amazing. It doesn't occur to you that a good percentage of the Eastern Seaboard drinks it. Must be kismet, must be fate, your eyes lock when you reach for the same brand high on the shelf (this is back before division of labor: grocery shopping is a field trip, the Laundromat is a night on the town). *You grew up on the heavenly coffee? You're kidding! Me too!* The next morning the can, yellow and black, hermetically sealed, makes that hiss when it's opened, smells like home, and comes with a cute little scoop. And now that you're a new couple and playing house—now that you know you drink the same coffee—you buy it three cans at a time, and keep them, of course. The scoops, that is. They accumulate in a wire basket that hangs from a nail over the kitchen sink, eventually spill into the corners of your world and take on lives of their own.

It's a quarter of a century later, having had to search one morning, having found it under a soup pot in the dish-drain (whew) that you realize—but one scoop remains.

It's green—a diminutive measuring cup—plastic, translucent, an inch deep, its diameter about the size of a half dollar. Chock full o'Nuts reads the handle: the letter F scripted, *fanciful*; the capital C a fingernail shaving, whereas the N for nuts is chunky and bold. Apparently made in Rahway, New Jersey—that's what it says on the flip side anyway—though on the bottom of the scoop, with no trace of irony comes the old slogan: *the heavenly coffee.*

And now you're on the prowl. You search drawers, cabinets, under the bathroom sinks, in the playroom for scoops. After all, they could be, they *should* be any/everywhere: they were that useful, their overall versatility not to be underestimated. They doubled, in their time, as dispensers of all manner of apothecary matter (Robitussin, milk of magnesia, boric acid), stood in for toy tea cups, building blocks, and Play-Doh molds. These tiny all-purpose shovels could excavate your whole history: met a guy, married him, raised a couple of kids, started every day—whatever happened the night before, whatever was planned or not for the day ahead—with a pot of coffee. Two cups per, he took sugar, you didn't, you went for fat free, he demurred, but every day you filled the kettle, poured the water into the grounds—four or five scoops' worth—this you could count on, this pot of coffee (always a Chemex, and how many of those glass beakers have you broken and replaced?) resolutely measured, sipped, gulped, or guzzled. This, at least in part, you realize now—now that there is but one scoop left to tell the tale—is what got you through. So. You dump bins, baskets, and boxes, ransack ribbons, magnets, dominoes, dice; sift through crayons, colored pencils, and finger-paints; empty old socks full of Scrabble letters and poker chips. You retrieve two Monopoly hotels, a baggie full of birthday candles, three silver dollars, two lobster picks, a marble that looks like the planet Earth, and a rectal thermometer. Not a scoop in the bunch.

You call your mother. *Do you remember those scoops that came in a can of Chock full o'Nuts?* you ask.

Your mother: They don't make them anymore.

You: Do you remember the colors?

She doesn't hesitate. She's certain they came in blue, green, and yellow.

You: Do you miss them?

Your mother: Not much.

She advises you that a scoop is the equivalent of two tablespoons, or an eighth of a cup. She has the very same measure in stainless steel, don't you?

Well, yes, of course (you're only a little defensive). It's aesthetically acceptable—but not practical. The handle is too long. Unwieldy. You can't leave it alone for a minute. It won't balance on the counter, tips over empty or full.

Why on earth would you need it to keep its balance? a person might ask. Well, you don't. Scooping is scooping, a continuous action, and even so, by virtue of the long handle, more than twice as long as the scoop itself, the scooper has less control than she should over the scooped. Whereas the scoops that came for *free* in every can of Chock full o'Nuts? They were perfectly designed for scooping, and balancing, collecting, and sorting. They came in primary colors, red included, it comes to you now, red very rare, and therefore coveted, in the way of an especially nifty surprise at the bottom of a box of cereal. *Why didn't you save a red one?*

You: Do you happen to know when they stopped making them?

Your mother: I haven't a clue.

With hope in your heart, you google Chock full o'Nuts to discover it's presently owned by the Massimo Zanetti Beverage company. You find you can make an inquiry through customer service. You write to ask what happened to the scoops.

Dear Dinah,

Thank you for taking the time to contact Massimo Zanetti Beverage Company.

Due to environmental concerns, we have discontinued putting a scoop in the containers to help reduce solid waste. However we will be most happy to send you some in the mail.

The note is signed by Melody from Customer Service. You're excited. You type fast and hit send.

> *Dear Melody,*
> *Are you actually still making the scoops? Do you, in fact, have leftover scoops?*
> *In what colors, please?*

Melody replies:

> *Dear Ms. Lenney,*

(Now you're Ms. Lenney: she's suddenly wary, you're a virtual stalker, lurking and dangerous.)

> *. . . there isn't anything in our paperwork that has information you are specifically seeking answers to. The scoops that we currently have available are white ones made specifically for our Hills Bros. Cappuccino and we have yellow ones for our regular ground coffees.*

White ones. Feh. And if the company is so worried about the environment why do they continue to make scoops for other brands? Clearly this is the party line, the decision to eliminate scoops made long before Melody came on the scene, and more likely to do with economic than environmental concerns. But how is it you didn't notice? You'd defected, that's how. You'd moved on to trendier brands: Starbucks, Peets, Intelligentsia. Whole beans vacuum-packed in heavy-duty bags. Even when you deigned to buy your coffee in a can, it was Café Bustelo, Illy, Medaglia D'Oro, none of whom were offering you something for nothing, but the look of them stacked in your pantry made you feel, what? Pretentious? No! Worthy! Urban. Urbane? Besides which, you had plenty of scoops at the time, more than you needed, more than you knew what to do with. Taking up room in back of the silverware drawer. Accumulating calcium deposits in the bathtub.

Meanwhile, back at the website: "Throw away the scoop!" says the on-line catalogue. "Each stay-fresh packet makes one pot (eight to ten cups) of New York's favorite coffee! A case contains forty-two 1.5 oz packets." Are you supposed to believe *this* idea is environmentally sound? Do you want to throw away your last little green scoop for premeasured packets of coffee? Would you order your scoops in bulk, all white, or all yellow, in the name of ecology? Don't they get it? It's not about having the scoops—it's about hope. Who isn't willing to eat the cookie to get to the fortune? Who doesn't buy Cracker Jacks just for the prize? For that psychological lift first thing in the morning, you might actually have come back to Chock full o'Nuts. For a whiff of possibility as much as the smell of the beans themselves—and, best of all, the delight of guessing with one eye closed (as if you didn't know what the day had in store) and the other one trained for that first glimpse of color beneath the grounds.

EGGS

LEAH TAUGHT ME to separate eggs. First a swift, clean break, and then this high-wire act: the halves cradled in the fingertips of each hand, shifting the yolk back and forth from shell to shell, and letting the white—clear and gooey—drip into the bowl, until nothing was left but that quivering yellow heart, which was thrown down the disposal, or slipped to one of the dogs, or saved for a hollandaise and poured over my broccoli at supper. Meanwhile, the whites, whipped to a froth, then to sturdy peaks, then molded and baked in the oven, and that's where the story comes in: how I was just five when I separated the eggs for my own birthday cake (or maybe I only watched and clapped from the counter). A picture somewhere, layers frosted in chocolate and decorated with faux mushrooms, as miraculous as the ones sprung up whole overnight after a rain, but fashioned from meringue—egg whites and sugar—and consequently disappointing. Too sweet and airy for me. Devoted as I was to dense and savory even then, I'd have been just as delighted to blow out my candles in a three-egg omelet.

But, I'm asking, don't we forget about eggs? Don't we talk about them

as if they're no big deal? Delicate though they are, hasn't their prepara-
tion—as default breakfast—become metaphor and evidence of ordinary
competence? *She can't even boil an egg*, we sneer, and the implication is
clear. So when my own son, sixteen years old, well over six feet tall—he
shaves! he drives!—asks me this morning if I'll boil him a few, break up
the toast in the bowl the way he likes, I realize: it's not that he needs me
to wait on him—it's only that he truly doesn't know how. I've witnessed
his enthusiasm in the kitchen: elaborate feasts involving mountains of
eggs—scrambled or fried—with ham, sausage, salami, varieties of breads
and spreads; the accompanying utensils at the ready—whisks, spatulas,
wooden spoons, graters; more than one frying pan going at once, even.
However, the fact of a *boiled* egg has him stymied. Entertained as I am by
his culinary athleticism (I've long since stopped wincing when he breaks
an egg into a pan), by the vigor with which he goes after his breakfast,
whacking it against the side of the skillet, leaving a trail of sticky white in
its wake, shell fragments, too—it never occurred to me to offer instruc-
tion. Long ago, in fact, with no thought to finesse, I taught him instead
the trick of removing those elusive little chippings. He's an expert now,
goes after them with another bigger piece of same; works like a charm
(or a magnet) every time.

But who knew? Who remembered? To prepare a soft-boiled egg from
start to finish is no simple task. To lift it from the water before the yolk
begins to cook is only a matter of timing, sure. But to crack it open without getting burned; to scoop it out without losing most of the white to
the membrane, the yolk to the counter; to get breakfast to the table before the yellow starts to congeal: it's worth a demonstration, isn't it? *I'll
teach you*, I say.

This morning's lesson then: Three four-minute-eggs with two slices
of toasted rye. *Watch*, I say, after the timer goes off; one purposeful snap
of the wrist at the edge of a blue and white bowl, then I scoop the shells
clean with a spoon. *Your turn*, I say. And this boy—this champion! (check
out the parade of trophies in the other room), is afraid of his egg. He
bites his lip, holds his breath, plays for time as if this really were the high
trapeze: gingerly, he taps . . . A glance in my direction. Tap, tap. Nothing.

C'mon now, I say, and I hand him the spoon. *Try with this.* And then a bludgeoning—a murderous act—and removing the edible portion is no less violent. My boy, very sober and with no small amount of deference, hands me the third egg.

"I'll butter the toast," he says.

TWO GUITARS

A MINOR, E minor, A minor, E minor... To D minor. To E major.
And back to A minor. My go-to progression. So easy to play. Although
watching my fingers move along her neck, it occurs to me that I don't
so much want to own the chords as to discover them. I'm pretending I
don't know where I'm going, or what they're made of, or how they arrive
note by note—as if to invent them each time—and this is also why, with
the other hand (my right), I'd rather pick than strum, and why I prefer
an arpeggio held, to a chord struck. Either way it's mysterious, isn't it—A
minor, E minor. Who would suppose that move, from one chord to the
next, could turn a person inside out? Could make her rue or remember?
And with six strings only—six strings stretched taut across an empty box.
Or more shapely than a box—voluptuous, even. But still.

Peer inside the hole—this one under my palm—and there's a parchment-
like rectangular label, a volcano etched in brown ink with Japanese
letters superimposed, and then, underneath them, *Takamine, Model
C123S*, the S in bold like so: S. Below the model number, in cursive—as
if written by hand—comes a promise, a guarantee, an implicit contract

of sorts: *Constructed with greatest care and conscience for the player of this guitar.* And in smaller letters, *Since 1962, Made in Japan.* Then the strings (three nylon, three steel), strung across her honey-colored face all the way to the frets—which narrow as they extend the length of her—attaching to six tuning pegs made of something like bakelite with extra sheen. She's badly strung (I've long forgotten how it's done exactly—have reneged, it would seem, as "the player," on my part of the bargain) and dusty; not along the length of the frets, but between the hole and the bridge, and toward the slender end of her neck. Even so, and though her face is scratched and smudged, she's pretty; but she's not the original, not the first, not the guitar on which I learned, the old Gibson that belonged to my mother, which is now retired to a case behind the piano downstairs. Somebody dropped that one a hundred years ago—twenty-two, to be exact—but though it can never again be properly tuned, neither can I throw it away.

My mother's Gibson—although I don't remember her playing it. Or where it was kept (or how it came to me); only that it saw me through summercamp, and high school, a European tour, four years of college, another five in New York City, and then made the trip to Los Angeles, where we'd been living for almost two years when I took it to an audition in 1986. The play, written by an Israeli named Joshua Sobol, was called *Ghetto;* a shot at a job at the Mark Taper Forum, where, as far as I could tell, only famous actors ever got parts. For this project, though, about Lithuanian Jews, artists and musicians who continued to perform during the Nazi occupation, the theater was looking for a large ensemble, including five women, one of whom would understudy the lead. A Klezmer band had been hired to join the cast on stage, and if we played, we were supposed to bring our instruments along to auditions. Here was my chance, I just knew it: I chose an old Yiddish folksong—A minor, E minor, A minor, D minor—tuned up the Gibson, and practiced for Fred again and again.

The morning of the audition, I sat on the edge of a metal chair facing the producers—also the director, casting director, playwright, stage manager. Fingers shaking, I plucked out the accompaniment: *On a wagon bound*

for market/ There's a calf with a mournful eye/ High above him there's a spar-
row/ Winging swiftly through the sky/ Dona, Dona, Dona, Do-oooo-na . . .

About the way I play: I recently learned, from a stranger who couldn't have known it would hurt my feelings—my having nervously sung in his presence (thinking my alto would wow)—that I don't grab the chords as I should; rather, I *find* them finger by finger, string by string, just barely in time. I realize I'm not much of a guitarist, of course not—but I didn't know in 1986, or else I didn't think it mattered. And back then I was right. It didn't. I heard my voice fill the room and float back to me, and afterwards the audible pause, warm, approving—sonorous—and knew I was in. A tiny part, almost nothing to say and nothing to do, in one of those shows (too long, too grim) that turn out to be more affecting for the actors than the audience. I didn't even land the understudy gig—it went to a petite soprano. Still, I was thrilled: a union job with a union sal-ary; six weeks of rehearsal and a three-month run at the most prestigious theater in Southern California. In my own mind, I'd arrived.

It was during our first tech rehearsal—hours and hours under the lights, fussing with cues and props and sets and wardrobe—that some-body let the Gibson fall from the stage. "I'm so sorry," she whispered into the hush that followed, placing the guitar in my arms. I was standing in front of a chair, I remember—put my foot on the seat, propped it on my knee, and strummed. And right away I knew, I heard: A minor. A desperate twist of the second key. E minor. Then the first. A minor. A minor, A minor. I went hot to the tips of my ears and behind my eyes: my mother's old Gibson was done for. That very night, the theater offered to replace it—the crack, long and jagged, turned out to be visible under bright light—but how to estimate its value? It was older than I (which seemed *old* at the time)—Leah had taken it to Sarah Lawrence in 1955 and I was born the following year. And yet. Though a Gibson—and, as far as I was concerned, an antique—it wasn't worth much. That's what they told me at the Guitar Center on Sunset Boulevard, where, overwhelmed by the varieties and not at all sure what I was supposed to want (easier, I've found, to inherit—or to covet a thing when it actually belongs to somebody else), I picked out the Takamine, similar in size, shape, and finish; comfortable in my arms and under my slow-moving hands. It was after that production that I all but stopped playing anyway, except for years later, when the kids were small, to entertain them when nothing else would do. "Learn three chords," Grandpa Charlie once said, "and you'll be able to play a hundred songs." That was also when he told me— about the piano (but he'd say it again about the Gibson)—that if I learned to play an instrument, I would always have a friend.

And he wasn't wrong: for haven't I said, I still have it—I have both of them—I have never in all these years been without a guitar. But although it's true that with just a few chords (maybe not three—maybe four or five) a person can stumble her way through the American songbook, she'll eventually tire of bluffing; become a more sophisticated listener, perhaps—more aware of her limitations, therefore, and consequently less able to amuse much less fool herself. Even if she could grab the chords, basic as they are, simple as they sound to her ear, she'll eventually give up. So I'd pretty much retired the Takamine, too—until Jake asked for lessons; although when he resisted her I didn't insist. Electric he wanted, electric he'd have. For a while then, he was all about amps, and plugging in, and we were all about closing doors and wincing and waiting him out. Until one day he found her all by himself, wedged in the corner, behind the Steinway but in front of the Gibson, just waiting to be discovered; to be lifted from her fake-fur-lined case; to be brought upstairs to his room, where she's lived ever since.

She's not a particularly good instrument, he's told me (as if I didn't know)—eventually he'll need something better, at which point, at least as sentimental as I, he'll make me promise not to give her away. (As if I would or could.) In the meantime, he likes the acoustic color, striated, vibrating in layers against his palm and the tips of his elegant fingers. Day after day, he sits in the half dark of dusk before he settles into his homework, and again, under the light of the bedside lamp when he's done for the night, picking, strumming, never mind who's listening— who's spying from the hall outside his room—he doesn't notice or care. Lips pushed forward, eyes half-closed, he's inside the music; swimming in the sound and the rhythm; surfing—that is catching and riding—that is *grabbing* each change (surprising, inevitable) like he means it. As for me—I wish I could explain to that man, the one who called my skills into question: I was never in danger of not finding the music, only wanting to convince myself that it had found me.

SCRIPT

TITLED IN A stiff and angular font: TERMINATOR: THE SARAH CONNOR CHRONICLES. Came with a letter, *Dear Colleague . . . fans' intense interest . . . crucial to protect . . . zero tolerance for revealing pages or ideas . . . any violation of . . . disciplinary action . . .* Displinary action. Yeesh. Well. At least this time I got a script. Last time I worked on one of these evidently top-secret prime-time shows, I was given only my *sides*, the scenes in which I had something to do or say. Honestly. As if these pages are so important, as if they're handed down from some government agency—as if anybody cares. And maybe they do, maybe I'm that out of touch. But used to be we didn't take ourselves so seriously. Or rather, we were supposed to take *ourselves* seriously—as actors, I mean. Used to be you were cast in a TV show, you got the whole script and you read it, or pretended to, in the name of context, which was essential, we assumed, to delivering a credible performance. But these days even the audition material is phony. Case in point: last Monday, when the sides arrived as an email attachment, I was evidently reading to play opposite a regular character called Stephanie. "Who is Stephanie?" I asked Fred, who's actually watched the show. He didn't know. Because—ah ha!—it turns out, there's no such person. Turns out—now that I've got the job, I know—my scenes are with Sarah Connor herself. However, last week, flipping through the pages (this role is sizable) it appeared Stephanie and I were very concerned about *another* character, not in the scene, called Abraham. Well, I wanted the job—a guest-star (good money, good billing)—wanted to give an informed and nuanced reading, so I called my agent: "Can they tell me who Abraham is before the callback, please, and what he is to me?" They couldn't. They couldn't, wouldn't, and didn't. Because it turns out *I'm* Abraham! Abraham in disguise!

⚶

The week before, I'd gone in for a different role on the show, the kind of part I usually play, a professional woman, a hypnotherapist this time—but after a while the gigs begin to blur, amounting as they do to a couple of scenes in an office, a courtroom, a prison, a bank—*middle-aged,* read the character description, and this case: *intelligent, kindly, warm.* Not that any of us waiting to audition were flattered or fooled. Any one of us could play this role, and one of us would, and the decision would be about as momentous as choosing a sandwich for lunch—today the tuna, tomorrow salami. And on the menu? Two blondes—one round, one slender—a diminutive Asian, a tall Latino, an African American woman whose face and voice were vaguely familiar, and me. Meanwhile, in the corridor at least a dozen men were lined up to read for *Eileen,* a woman (a.k.a. Abraham!)—one guy in heels and a polka dot shift; another in a pencil skirt, gray with black trim, the jacket thrown over his arm; a third wore a turban, and lipstick, too orange: the Gay Pride parade right there outside casting in Building 138 on the second floor. Sorry, guys—nobody more surprised than I when the role came to me, though I shouldn't have been. For one thing, it's easier to turn a woman into a man than the other way around. For another—tall, dark, and handsome as I am, and having started on the boards at Waukeela Camp for Girls—I'm accustomed to playing the boys. I was Billy in *Carousel,* Captain Von Trapp in *The Sound of Music*—I came *this* close to winning the role of the King in *The King and I*. Lost out to a senior, but only because she was a senior. At thirteen I was a much more convincing Yul Brynner than she, but the director (a theater studies major at Smith) decided I had one more summer to shine.

△

Old wounds, old injustices—shake them off, old girl—focus on this script, copied off from what you know from experience were multi-colored drafts: white for the first, then pink, then blue, then orange, then green—each color signifying a new version and every change marked with an asterisk in the right-hand margin of the page. This one here, hot off the press, late-breaking in tasteful gray, is the final draft. Except you know better: words will change on the spot. Mid-scene, actors will shake their heads and call for writers; writers will come down from production, looking like writers, looking like they crawled out from under rocks, pale as grubs, and nearly as impervious. Remember cutting an earthworm in half and watching each end wiggle away? Were they silently screaming and we just didn't know? Television writers are not quite so cavalier. In fact, just this afternoon in the makeup trailer—where I was fitted for a fall, long and wavy—a call came in from one of those writers: she was on her way over, she wanted a look at the woman playing the man playing the woman. "Sorry, can't wait," I said, and skadoodled, suddenly self-conscious, besides which I really was running late. I grabbed up my script and raced to my car: made it to John Marshall High School just in time to pick up Jake and take him to a guitar lesson, and then out for sushi—just he and I (his sister and his father out of town)—where we ran my lines over an order of hijiki and a couple of kamakazi rolls.

On the way home, playing my real life part for all I was worth, I was moved to chide the boy about his priorities, even though back in the restaurant, he'd been generous enough to read all the other roles. Not easy to be tough with this child, who is funny and good. But school comes first, I insisted, so he would not have time to play two hours of tennis after dinner, not having casually mentioned a Spanish test scheduled for the following morning. Had he thought I didn't hear him? Had he supposed, preoccupied as I was, I wouldn't care? "I'm saying," he argued, "that some things are more important to me than school. I'm telling you because I want us to have an open and honest relationship."

"And I'm telling you," I answered, "because I, too, want for us to be open and honest with each other: sorry, pal, I'm not with that program."

Who wrote these lines? How to play this scene convincingly? I pretend I don't doubt myself; I pretend I wouldn't tweak this script and start again from the top if I could. I pretend I don't mind when Jake goes silent at the light at the corner of Glendale and Allessandro; gets out of the car in our driveway as fast as he can; sidles past me and into the house without meeting my eye; goes into his room and closes the door. Left alone in the kitchen, I shrug—for nobody's benefit. This—this is acting.

The evening crawls and I hope my boy is having a better time of it than I—with himself, with his text; for me, distracted as I am and full up with rue, the lines just aren't sticking. Two scenes to shoot tomorrow, which means I won't see him in the morning. He'll have to get his own breakfast, since I'll be up and out in the dark for an early set call. All day long, I'll be me and not me. First—face scrubbed in the mirror—the woman I am. Next, brows brushed up, lips lightened, hair slicked: me as a man. Then—that man as a woman—expertly spackled and coiffed, looking less like myself than like one of those guys in drag at the casting call. Bottom line, tomorrow when I'm all dressed up as Abraham or Eileen, no one will know that I haven't a clue how I got to be where I am, who I am; that I'm wanting to know how the story ends—and wanting it never to end, this story, the one where Fred and I got married and decided to stay in Los Angeles and had these two kids and managed to get them this far (or was it they who coaxed us along?) and now—now they will choose their own paths, make their own mistakes, as we did, as we continue to do. Nobody will know, to watch me on the set, that I'm thinking back to this evening's scene with my real life boy; wondering about his Spanish test, his after school plans, his dinner, and is he all right? Will he be all right for the rest of time? Does he realize I've been improvising? That though I act with conviction, as if I know how to be all grown up in this world, I am—I have always been— making it up as I go?

How is it that life gets more baffling, not less? Nobody told us, did they. It's about running out of options, I suppose—you wouldn't think it, but the narrowing of the road in the middle of the map is confusing and scary. That being so, on this night in this house, turns out one of us is more sure than the other; young enough to be sure for us both. Jake doesn't scrutinize his coordinates—he isn't asking how he got here. Whether or not we decide to be parents, we don't choose to be somebody's daughter or son; we don't delude ourselves, not most of the time, that we could have arrived on the planet some other way. Therefore Jake doesn't question his right, or mine, to play our parts. What a relief, and how reassuring, when he finally opens his door and comes downstairs to find me, his mother (*that's who I am*); when he collapses sideways on the big bed, head and feet hanging off the ends, and offers to make us a cup of tea. When he suggests—not in the least as if it were scripted—that perhaps I'd like some more help with my lines.

CHRISTMAS TREE

"DON'T YOU LOVE Christmas?" asks Jake. He starts asking before Thanksgiving, and tortures me straight through the new year; this a time-honored ritual in and of itself, *Don't you love Christmas, Mom?*

I do not, I say every time.

And when he insists, *Yes, you do, Mom, you love Christmas, say you do*, I stick to my lines. I'm denying it, see, I'm making my point: it's not that I object to Christmas, exactly. It's only that it feels a little like Halloween to me—or like a game of charades. It's not mine to love.

"Don't be ridiculous," says Fred. "Of course it's yours to love. Christmas is for everyone."

Easy for him to say.

Growing up we didn't do Christmas. We celebrated Chanukah, with the restraint befitting a minor Jewish holiday; a simple menorah, brisket and latkes, and, in concession to the season, a few understated gifts. But no decorating—no blue and silver banners, no blue and white lights; no point in competing with all that tinsel—we knew we were Jews and we couldn't have Christmas, my siblings and I (though we grew up *Christmas-adjacent*, in a town with a church on every corner; the garden club, restricted, just beyond the pachysandra that bordered our front lawn). Instead, we braced ourselves, kept a low profile, and waited out the festivities. And what a relief come the new year, when the Christmas lights came down, and our house looked like a house among houses again, not somehow emaciated and bereft. Meanwhile, Christmas was fraught for me not only because we were the only Jews in town, but because I left town to spend the day on the other side of the Hudson with my father, who'd remarried a woman named Noel. "Merry Christmas," he'd boom, as I came through the front door year after year, then feigned injury when I rolled my eyes. "That's not nice," he'd say. And maybe it wasn't. But I had a photo of my dad at thirteen, standing over his Torah portion, wearing a fringed tallit; who did he think he was kidding?

Eventually I married my own true WASP. Not that he was religious, not a bit, but Fred grew up with Christmas and all the trimmings. So holiday season '86, the year we were wed, we bought a skinny live tree—as if we meant to plant it—as if the occurrence of Christmas that week were a coincidence, and why not decorate just for fun, afterwards we could dig it a hole. I hung dangly earrings from the branches, strung them with garlands of saved paper ribbon, curled with a scissors. And the next few years—how did we celebrate? With friends and family, I suppose. But when Eliza was born, I put the kibosh on Christmas—for good, I said— as was, I announced, my right and my responsibility. No big deal for a gentile to attend a seder, I explained to Fred, to dance the horah at somebody's bar mitzvah; but some kind of disgrace to be a Christmas-loving Jew. Perfectly commendable, I reasoned, for a Christian to acquaint himself with my traditions; whereas, when the likes of me takes on Christmas, she's a fraud, an imposter, and a hypocrite. *We will not do Christmas,* I said. Never mind that Fred had valiantly donned a yarmulke on more than one occasion; that he'd been willing to learn the Sabbath blessings (though, if left to his own devices he still veers off into "Red River Valley"); there wouldn't be tit for tat, not from now on. I didn't care that it wasn't about religion for him; only peace on earth, Santa Claus, and the smell of pine—the whiff of childhood—in his very own living room. In the end he gave in: What else could he do in the face of such sanctimony?

And so that year, just weeks before Eliza's first birthday—we sat around awkward and sad. Fred's parents were dead. My own were on the other coast. Our little girl, seemingly oblivious to his melancholy and my misgivings, played by herself on the kitchen floor. Watching her, it came clear to me: she was every bit as entitled to Christmas as she was to my mishegas. How dare I steal the holiday from him? How dare I steal her legacy from her? I was ashamed. And just like that, I gave up the cause.

But once you surrender to Christmas, it's a slippery slope; you can't do it half-assed. You can't hang a scrawny tree with costume jewelry. You need one of those jobs that takes over the living room and molts needles all over the coffee table; you need ornaments to weigh it down—one of a kind ornaments—as if you'd inherited them, as if you'd come by them honestly. You need lights, lots of lights, and hand-knit stockings, and jingle bells, and candy canes. Before I knew it, I was hanging wreaths, decorating cookies, writing letters to Santa, leaving out milk and cookies, and a carrot for Rudolph. *What are you?* somebody asked Eliza when she was in kindergarten. *I'm half Jewish and half Christmas*, she said without pause.

Tradition thus established, these last few years, I've reverted, as the elderly do, to my curmudgeonly ways. I'm free now to be the bristly, conflicted, slightly sheepish American Jew I am, expected by this point to make certain noises, to play cynic and skeptic. Hence our routine, Jake's and mine: *Mom, don't you love Christmas?* he teases from under his lashes. *Yeah, yeah, yeah*, I say. But if I'm a grump, I'm not the Grinch. I'm not about to steal Christmas from my children—I gave it to them in the first place, right? It was my idea.

And what's my reward? Why, kids—young people, that is—who love Christmas. Young people, related to me, who revel in this holiday without embarrassment or confusion; people who, if they question who they are or what they're doing—and they will (don't we all)—who, if they focus on their perceived shortcomings and failures, who, if they carry remorse or regret, will at least not bear the weight of historical or cultural obligation.

So: it's coming on Christmas. Eliza is home for the holidays, our last all together before Jake leaves for college next fall, which makes this an especially poignant time. The tree is in its place—in the corner by the window that faces the street. As usual, I instructed them to choose something unobtrusive. As usual, they picked the biggest they could manage, a noble fir, fragrant and full and tall. It's strung with white lights for now (that's one of my tasks), but otherwise bare. On the Eve, Fred will put on the Weavers' Christmas album, as his parents did when he was small. Then, while I sing along from the sink or the stove or the counter, he and kids will decorate. And afterwards—never mind their objections—I'll swoop in to make sure the baubles are evenly distributed. Between the glass birds and bears and fishes and fruits and beetles and balls, I'll find room for my favorites: hand-crafted in school by one child or the other; crudely shaped—painted or baked—out of dough (red) or construction paper (green), and trimmed with foil or glitter or pieces of doily. And after the holiday? I'll wrap every trinket in tissue and stow them together in a bin, along with the stockings (and the menorah), and a little brass angel that belonged to Fred's mother, whom I never knew, though I am the keeper of her things, too. But I'm getting ahead of myself. At some point before I put everything away—sometime between Christmas and New Year's—Jake will find me rearranging again; or sweeping the needles; or on my knees watering the tree at its base. *Mom, you love Christmas,* he'll say. I'll harumph, as is called for in the script, then turn on the lights, and together we'll watch them brighten as dusk turns to dark.

BREAKFRONT

IT ARRIVED IN four pieces—except the word "pieces" doesn't do the job. It arrived in four—four what? Four parts? Four boxes—each one wider and heavier than I, than either of us; and it was just us back then, just Fred and I in our new house—our first house (our first and our last, could that be?); the one in which we'd all grow up (not just the kids); the one in which we two will get old (along with the dogs). This house, this one, which—having expanded like an accordion—has now contracted again, is now, as it was then, just the right size for us and this dog—the last dog (we tell ourselves she's the last, though neither of us believe it, not really). The point is it came in four boxes. Who knew they made boxes that big? And how did we even get them in the front door? We didn't—we couldn't have—it must have been the moving men—three of them—who hoisted the boxes from their truck, heaved them inside, left them in the middle of the room, and drove away. In this house, see, there's no foyer, no mudroom, no front or back hall—open the door, step inside, soft-shoe to your right, and you're sitting on the arm of the sofa.

Let me say that I knew right away: we weren't keeping it. Disassembled to fit in four boxes, it would never fit in this house. It had once lived in my grandmother's dining room in the grand old Tudor in Teaneck, New Jersey—one of those houses set back from the street on a manicured lawn. There was a willow tree at the far end of the driveway, and a huge rhododendron out front, and inside, landings, corridors, banisters, moldings; whereas, we, proud new owners of a low-slung Spanish bungalow on the east side of Los Angeles . . . what were we to do with a breakfront, packed up and sent by my mother not long after my grandmother's death?

And why did we call it a breakfront anyway? It wasn't one, really—no requisite protruding center section when all of a piece. What *is* it? I ask my mother on the telephone just the other day. I persist as if it still matters; as if, with the right name, it might finally shift into proper focus and place. What is it called? "Well, shelves," she says. "Bookshelves. Or a china cabinet. Not a breakfront, no, not strictly speaking." A credenza, I've now decided, having googled and perused the images, that's what it is, though the name alters nothing, and though it feels strange, almost traitorous, to call it anything other than what it's always been called: this monstrous piece of furniture, part of a dining room set that belonged to my grandmother's mother, with which my mother was unwilling to part.

As timing would have it, it arrived a scant week before the Madame herself was due to visit. *The Madame*—this is what Ron affectionately calls my mother—designer, chef, and self-described aficionado of culture, art, taste. When I called to tell her, "Mom, I'm selling it—it won't fit, not ever, it won't"—she answered, "Just wait, I'm coming." And when I said, "Mom, I really don't want this thing, it has nothing to do with who I am," she said, "Dinah, I'll be there in just a few days . . ."

So—did we take the pieces out of the boxes? Rather, did we cut the packing away so as to have a real look? We must have. Which had to have been how I knew I didn't want it—its bases, dark-stained, American black walnut (very rare, Leah tells me just the other day), and ornately carved, with angry little skulls for knobs; and the shelves set behind beveled glass, five of them in each case, and each case over five feet tall, meant to stand on top of those heavy bottoms which came up to my waist, understand, and which, when pushed together, called for a room twice as big as any in our house, and not a wall high or wide enough to be had. But even if there were, I didn't want it—I'd never have chosen it, grand and grown-up as it was—and why did I have to wait for my mother to confirm that was so?

Why oh why had she sent it to me? I'd have been so pleased, really I would, to inherit one of Grandma's nice Chinese tureens, or a pair of silver candlesticks. Who'd ever want a breakfront?

The Madame arrived on a Friday afternoon, with time enough to take a nap before the opening of *Blame It on the Movies*, a musical revue in which I was appearing in a tiny theater on Santa Monica Boulevard—a triumph of an evening—and afterwards a party on the stage—with champagne, and smoked salmon, and new potatoes halved and adorned with crème fraîche and fake caviar; and there were toasts, of course, and lavish kvelling besides: "Never," said a casting director whom I only slightly knew—gripping both my hands in his, batting his lashes overtime— "Never have I been so excited about an actor, not since . . ." Yadda yadda, on and on he went. About my performance. In *Blame it on the Movies*. In which I sang, and sort of danced and, I am proud to say, hula-hooped my way through an entire musical number (not that I can tell you why or what it was called)—and this praise, effusive as it was, delivered in front of my mother.

And so, when we arrived home after midnight—flopped down in our respective chairs on opposite sides of the room with the breakfront in pieces between us, so that we had to crane our necks to have a conversation; when she got suddenly quiet, bit her lower lip the way she does, and squinted in my general direction—well she had something to tell me, clearly, and I, leaning out on the edge of my seat to catch her eye, her gaze, was eager to hear whatever it was, because I supposed—what did I suppose? That she finally recognized and appreciated the range and significance of my natural gifts?

"What are you thinking, Mom?" I asked.

A pause. A pause as big as a packing box. She did that thing she does with her mouth—lips pushed forward into a smile, no teeth—a good indication that she's several steps ahead of us all.

"I'm thinking," she said, "about the furniture."

⚘

Convince me, if you can, that all this isn't about a woman who, though there is a continent between them, cannot get out from under her mother. Tell me, can you?—that I shouldn't have understood, whatever talent I possessed notwithstanding, that my mother wasn't wrong to be skeptical about the wisdom of my presumed vocation; that I shouldn't have anticipated that the person I'd grow up to be would have to improvise straight through middle age, never mind the furniture, though it's true that the breakfront turns out to be a metaphor, and elastic as such: not just solid and defining of the literal and figurative interior, but a reminder that it behooves us all to reframe and reinvent whenever we can.

"Dinah, good design is not about buying new things," my mother said that night, when I winced, or gasped, or audibly snorted. Not so much as a word about my having mastered a time step (and what about those scrumptious canapés? And how about the standing ovation?). "Good design," she continued, "is about making use of heirlooms," as if we hadn't, both of us, just spent the evening in the theater.

"Well, I really believe that," she muses on the phone, when I quote her.

"But do you remember that night?" I ask.

"Of course I do," she says, evidently tickled. "I am very creative," she adds, and both of us laugh.

Sometimes (often, in fact) this woman inside the receiver sounds just like my mother—though, I'm embarrassed to admit, it has only recently occurred to me that it's I who am guilty of conjuring her and not the other way around. She isn't the person I've yearned for and imagined— why should she be? She is, rather, her singular self, in spite of my projecting and endowing and wanting and needing and expecting her to conform to my version of her. How unfair I have been, when all along she has rightfully had an inner life and a script all her own. Now, talking about the breakfront hurtles her back; she is telling me about visiting her grandmother in a cavernous apartment on West End Avenue, how, in childhood, she was abandoned there for a whole afternoon and evening, put to sleep in "a maid's room" and woke up in the dark, and was frightened, young and small as she was, and why on earth had they left her there; and where was her grandmother? "Well," sighs. "She probably didn't like children any more than my own did."

⟁

We moved the breakfront into place that night. My mother directed us, Fred and me, and we grunted and strained and humped it across the room: first, the bases, to either side of the fireplace, where they're hardly noticeable, as if they've always been there. And the shelves? We pushed them up against the opposite wall, though not before we turned them over, as instructed and with my mother excitedly hovering, so they'd be self-standing. For years—for twenty-five years—I've intended to stain the bottoms, which, narrow as they are, made better tops; have been the tops for twenty-five years. As if this were about me and my intentions. As if I don't turn out to be a supporting player in this story, and not the star at all. See, tall as the shelves are, you'd have to get on your toes to discover that the wood isn't finished; you'd have to know your furniture to realize that they're balanced on their heads, or to notice that the brass keyholes in the tattersall doors are actually upside down. Someone would have to alert you to my living room set as stand-alone, as a showpiece in a former life—but you'd need only a hint or two to figure out how to put it together again.

To have taken it apart, to have given it a second act, around which all kinds of drama, more and less predictable, continues to unfold? You'd be some kind of brilliant.

SPICE CHEST

MUSTARD, NUTMEG, GINGER, *Pepper, Cinnamon, Allspice, Bay-Leaves.* A miniature dresser—perhaps cherry or pine. All those years at Waukeela Camp for Girls. All those nature walks, all those leaves pressed between the pages of the *Big Book of Knowledge,* and even so I don't know my oaks from my elms from my maples, not after they've been turned into furniture. Whatever it is, this wood, it's stained golden, grimy in places, at the corners, along the edges. If I took a rag to it, and some Murphy Oil Soap, it would come clean; if I rubbed at the rusty, old screws in the center of the porcelain knobs with a bit of metal polish they'd turn out to be what? Brass? Nickel? I don't know my metals, my elements, my trees. But I know my spices.

Each little drawer is labeled just so with a miniscule plaque, not as long or as wide as my thumb; the letters, also blackened with age, pressed into a metal scroll. Six tiny boxes, two by two, side by side, except for *Bay-Leaves* on the bottom, a single drawer that extends the length of the base, twice the size of the others. This chest, it's a gift from my mother, and I want to say it sat on a stainless steel shelf on the back of the stove in the house I grew up in. Or—or was it on the Formica counter, next to the cake stand? (And always half a cake under the bell: pound, lemon, Viennese plum.) Did it rest against the length of butcher block? On the window sill between the creamers and the crockery? Could we see over it into the garden? Past the tall fence and the Nicholson's honeysuckle hedge, across their backyard and all the way to their sun porch? Wherever it lived when I was a kid, once grown up and in a house of my own, I wanted it all for myself, and asked. "I'm not ready to part with it," my mother said. And I was surprised. (Though I wouldn't be now—now that Eliza has the flight jacket among other things—and is eyeing and admiring items I'm not yet inclined to give away.) Why did *she* need it? I wondered. What for? Then, years later, when I'd long since outgrown this brand of kitsch—at a point in my life when I fantasized a bonfire in the back yard, wanted to clear every surface, to blow it all up, to do me and mine over in spare and muted—it turned up on a UPS truck, in a box full of Styrofoam peanuts; for a birthday, must have been, and I took it downstairs to my office, placed it on the Parson's table there, an em-dash between two rows of books.

Mustard, Nutmeg, Ginger, Pepper, Cinnamon, Allspice, Bay-Leaves. Who made this little chest, with its perfect little drawers? (see how they slide in and out without sticking or jamming?) Who thought it up? And why these spices? What about parsley, sage (rosemary and thyme), cumin, and saffron? Where to keep tarragon and cream of tartar; marjoram, vanilla bean, clove, and paprika, hot and sweet? As if I'd keep any of those in a mock chest of drawers: my spices, mostly in little glass jars, congregate in the cabinet above the microwave (catty corner to the coffee cups, and below the good china), caps screwed on tight to keep them pungent and uncorrupted. My cupboard imitates my mother's, if not very well: ill-behaved rows of spices on one side (there isn't room for them all!); bottles (oils and vinegars) on the other; and beside the stove, a heavy jar of coarse kosher salt and a tall wooden peppermill much like hers.

So—if not spices—what did she keep in this chest for all those years? What do I keep in it now? Coins for starters. Old silver dollars, four of them, and a fifty cent piece from 1924. Also a penny, dated 1902, over a hundred years old. Pounds and shillings jumbled in there, souvenirs from an overnight in London, when, with Eliza in tow, I spent far too much pretty money (overlarge and printed in pastels) on cabs, and ended up with all this change. Marbles. Three green marbles behind *Cinnamon*—I suspect they're only inside the drawer because I picked them up off the floor at some point and had to stow them somewhere. Baby teeth in the *Ginger* compartment, but only two of them: whose are they? My daughter's? My son's? And why did I keep just these two in a bit of green tissue, since I'm certain I threw the rest away in some kind of rebellion—having saved them at first only because my mother saved mine (but not out of nostalgia; she'd actualy had some project in mind). Last I heard of them— pointy little pearls (if they looked like these) and yellow at the root—she'd taken them out of a jewelry pouch to prove there was no such thing as a tooth fairy. "Poor Leah," whispered Eliza, who was six at the time. "She doesn't believe in magic." Also filed under *Ginger*, keys to the safe deposit box at the Bank of America on Glendale, where we keep the wills, and the living wills, and savings bonds, a cameo that's much too grand for me, and a dragonfly, all rubies and diamonds (also inherited) that's much too delicate.

Back to the chest: back to *Nutmeg* and *Allspice* and *Bay-Leaves*: hooks for picture frames, a few stray buttons, sea glass, brown and blue, a Rilke poem, copied out and folded in thirds; an old chapstick, a raquet dampener, a purple guitar pick, the tile S worth one point from an ancient Scrabble set, an acorn, and Jake's face the size of a postage stamp and glued onto a piece of wood meant for a key chain: full-cheeked, baby teeth intact.

But *Pepper* is empty. Empty. How can that be? Nothing but boxes and drawers and jars and pots and bowls and baskets in this house. And something in the back or the bottom of every one, from paperclips to hairclips to pushpins to brooches to single earrings to single socks to business cards to birthday cards: from old jacks to old balls to broken ornaments, broken pottery, broken gadgets and chargers: from extension cords to pieces of yarn, from ribbons to paint swatches—and if all or any of it meant something once upon a time, if I saved these things for reasons, I've long ago mostly forgotten what they were. I don't discriminate, no system at work, no method to the madness. So here, in the mug at my right, pencils, pens, two screwdrivers, a plastic ruler, and a sterling silver candle snuffer. And to my left, in the file box, addresses and phone numbers of friends (dear and not so dear), and family (dead and not so dead)—the five-by-eight-inch cards pressing up against each other as if they were equals, as if they were equally important and equally easy to locate: the information, and the people themselves.

Pepper, though, is light in my palm, smooth and finished under the plaque, and rough where the back of the drawer meets the frame. *Pepper*, dusty in the corners, smells not remotely of pepper, smells like nothing but wood—but not just wood. Like memory—it smells like memory—like the deep bottom of something somewhere. Like time itself, nothing but time to play with marbles, and coins, and keys, and buttons; under the piano, in the window seat, on the stairs, in the cedar closet—at the kitchen table with my mother just there, chopping bunches of parsley, stirring a sauce, organizing her pantry; we two keeping company on a raw afternoon, and the lamps lit, and the sky growing dark, turning the light inside yellow and warm. Sniff *Pepper*: it's as though I've stowed my mother for safekeeping. I might as well have my nose in her neck—isn't that her soap on the air? The faintest whiff of her perfume? But though she gave it to me, though it brings her close, though I loved it because it was hers, it was never she who filled this chest—not back then anyway, not so I knew it. I wanted it because it was part of a game, my game, a world of my making; my own belongings in and out of these little drawers, in and among and transforming my mother's, as my mother herself has always been in and among and defining of mine.

JEANS AND CLOGS

IN THIS DREAM the other night, I was somewhere in the city. It's always the city—New York, I mean—always night or overcast, dark and wet, familiar but not, and I'm always wearing the wrong shoes or no shoes at all. In this particular dream—well, let's just call it what it was—in this *nightmare* my hair was pulled back in a ponytail (fetching), and I wore something sleeveless with sparkles (say what?), and white patent sandals (I have never in my life owned such things), and it was snowing, of course, coming down fast. Weirdly, too, in the dream, I thought I looked good; I was pleased with the hair and the dress, though the shoes were a problem, not only cheap and scuffed (I noticed—this is the sort of thing I notice in my dreams), but all wrong for navigating treacherous stairs and alleys, and me, just off of work—as a waitress, mind you (though I last waited tables in Manhattan in 1984)—running, tripping, slipping, sliding, desperate to find a cab, hopelessly lost and late, just about out of time, as I generally always am in the dreams.

The thing is, this purgatory? This is not my New York. By day anyway, I pine for the city—or maybe I'm pining for myself in that time and space, maybe that's what it is. Last time we were there and down in the village, a jewel of a day, I was wearing what I always wear, what I've been wearing for the last two decades or so: jeans and clogs. But how did it come to this? Nightmare garb aside, what did I do with my bohemian self? With the girl who, straight through the '80s, wore parachute pants in every color (from Canal Jeans), and leg warmers to match, and jaunty hats and crazy scarves and enormous hoops in her ears, and jazz shoes or tall boots with high heels, depending? When did I permanently surrender to undergraduate garb (see, we all wore jeans and clogs in the '70s), and when did undergraduate garb come to define me as the definitely middle-aged person I am?

Periodically, I resolve to change it up. To finally become the woman I intended to be—was on the way to being. I waltz into the Eileen Fisher store on Colorado in Old Town Pasadena and finger the very fine fabrics, only to check the tags and skulk away; or, more likely, I order up a storm from a catalogue (J. Peterman or the Peruvian Collection), to invariably find that the clothes are heavier and boxier than they appear in the pictures: this isn't a dress, I tell the mirror, it's curtains—or slip-covers, that's what this is, and this, and this. In a fury I return every item, because, as I write under "comments," if I'd wanted to be upholstered I'd have gone to Raymond, the guy on Sunset between Lucile and Micheltorena, who did my sofa.

Truth is, though, I've about given up on any notion of myself as chic or hip or happening: jeans and clogs it is—all-jeans-all-clogs-all-the-time. And in this house, which claims just that one long mirror on the inside of my son's upstairs closet; in this Los Angeles neighborhood where I don't do much metropolitan walking (and am therefore unlikely to catch more than glimpse of my full-length reflection just before the automatic doors part for me at the grocery store), I'm mostly unaware of the figure I make. It's not that I'm wholly deluded, but I've persuaded myself I can pull it off—am only occasionally reminded, as when a colleague turns up in belted trousers and tasteful pumps (making me feel at once too young and too old), that I didn't grow up to be my mother, or any of the other glamorous New Yorkers I supposed I'd eventually be.

⚖

That recent afternoon in Manhattan the weather was warm for November and we dined, Fred and I, with our twentysomething daughter in a bistro on a cobblestone street east of Broadway. On our way to the restaurant, Eliza peered into the windows of the brownstones with palpable longing, and we salivated, all three of us, to think of her living in the city in a walk-up apartment—to imagine our girl a bona fide New Yorker, with a bathtub in the kitchen, a geranium on the fire escape, and a compact umbrella in full-time residence at the bottom of her backpack.

Once settled at the table, we ordered omelets and salads and beer and café au lait in bowls, and took our time over lunch, reminiscing about that era three decades earlier, when we, her parents, had known the neighborhood well. We told stories about taxi drivers and parties and weather and work—about the subway and the crosstown bus—about the Greek diner on Madison where we splurged on breakfast; and P. J. Clark's and the White Horse Tavern and the Cookery and the Oyster Bar in Grand Central Station where we slurped chowder at the counter—New England for him, Manhattan for me; about the NYPL, where we met (but not in the stacks, no, we had day jobs there, both of us), and the reservoir where we jogged most mornings; about the Zoo, and the Frick, and the Met, and MoMA. About how, though he hadn't yet given up his own place, Fred had just about moved in with me—had managed to find a hanger for his suit in the back of my overstuffed closet (what happened to all those parachute pants?), and a spot for his shaving cream in my medicine chest—only weeks before we got on a plane to Los Angeles to take the working vacation from which we never returned.

Eventually, all talked out and suddenly aware of the time, we paid the check and gathered our things—Fred and I on our way to the airport, Eliza headed back to Boston and school. Stepping out on the sidewalk, I blinked against the afternoon sun and turned my gaze to the storefront window, where I saw reflected this purposeful beauty—leggy, gamine—a girl striding forward in tall leather boots. Eliza, of course—her step, not quite in sync with my own, should have been my first clue. Instead, as if confused, I touched my hand to the back of my head to find my hair cropped close; whereas hers wouldn't be tamed, blew out behind her, glinting, the last of her to disappear into the bricks of the adjacent building. *Where did she go?* I wondered. How had she gotten away from me, moved as I'd been to stop and stare and admire? And that's when I noticed the woman behind her in jeans and clogs, who turned then and quickened her pace to catch up with one girl and leave the other behind.

POSTER

THE FUNNY PART is that he's smoking. As if Whitney would ever have put a cigarette between his lips. Mr. Milk Mustache. Mr. Half-a-Beer with dinner. Mr. Brush-for-a-full-two-minutes. Maybe a *clove* cigarette—definitely, if the part called for it. Whit would have done anything to play a role authentically and well.

In the poster of a person looking at a poster, it's Whitney, and yet it isn't at all. A man in a suit and hat and shoes, all taupe, including his face—but for the white squares at his cheekbones and the black smear of a mustache—against a flat, brown background. White again, the suggestion of cuffs and collar, and a sliver of tomato-red for his tie. The shapes like construction paper scraps, the contours defined, a cut-out man, a featureless paper doll, a mannequin, but Whitney even so. Whit's posture, the length of him, the slump of his shoulders, the thrust of his neck. Whit—not quite disappeared—in the picture of a man looking at a picture. Things disappearing into things disappearing into things. This poster for a gallery in Berkeley, California (the black letters themselves framed—underneath the man in the hat—in a red that matches his tie), is significant for me because I know the model and because I knew the artist, too, once upon a time. There's his name in black script between the model's heels: *Newton*.

△

Once, a non-union actor in my twenties, I spent two summers with a repertory company called the Weathervane Theatre in Whitefield, New Hampshire. That's where I met Whit, the company leading man, tall and so painfully thin it hurt to watch him bend his knees. He'd grown up in adjacent Vermont, wore khakis frayed at the hem, polo shirts in pastel colors, and topsiders. Sharp-nosed and blue-eyed, he had fine brown hair, a small head atop narrow shoulders, that long neck; he was the definition of patrician. Who'd have known his father was a beer-guzzling drunk? Who'd have supposed his mother was provincial? His brother a fuck up, his sister as conventional as it's possible to be? Whit looked to me like everything I thought I couldn't have.

The company, actors and crew, lived and worked and ate and slept in this big old rundown house on top of a hill: The Spruces. In the evenings, after all-day rehearsals on the wide, wraparound porch, after building and painting sets on the lawn, or working through the music on an out-of-tune upright piano in the dining room, we piled into cars and went to the theater to perform. Afterwards, we came back to the house, sat in clumps on the dead grass, drank from a keg, watched fireflies, slapped at mosquitoes. I was in love half-a-dozen times each summer, but never so crazy about anybody as I was about Whit, who was crazy for somebody else, of course. He loved Emma. A Southerner, a redhead, a company member before my time, she'd gone on to a cabaret gig in another city. I only met her once. She was boisterous, a belter with boobs—not at all right for my Whit, whom I pictured with a white-gloved debutante, blond and narrow-lipped, who would come to the relationship with a hope chest and sterling silver service for twelve. But Emma and Whit were an item, practically engaged, hence I was his default buddy for two summers running.

Long before I joined the company, Whit had become acquainted with a couple who lived down the road, Roslyn Locke and Geoff Newton. Geoff was an artist, Roslyn a bookbinder by trade though she wanted to write. They lived in a square little house with their toddler, a towhead called Wren. Often, mother and daughter posed for Geoff. I have six *Newtons*, myself, and three of them feature one or the other—from the side, from behind, faceless and featureless, but undeniably Roslyn and Wren in flat, saturated hues and in wholesome scenes. A child playing or listening to a story, a woman studying or reading a book. But not in this poster, no. This is man of the world with a fedora and a smoke— my Whitney, the actor—elegantly slouching, one hand in his pocket, the other holding the picture in the picture, that cigarette dangling, that hat angled just so. And though Geoff didn't work in detail, somehow even Whit's facial features are evident in the way the nose is lighted—highlighted—and in the downward slant of his glance.

That second summer—thanks to Roslyn and Geoff who had neighbors vacationing out of town—Whit and I were offered a place for a week in exchange for watching their farm. We took the job, a chance to get away from The Spruces—from mystery casseroles topped with cornflakes—a chance to sleep in real beds with real blankets. We played house together, invited Geoff and Roslyn for dinner; got up in the morning and fed the animals; picked cucumbers from the garden, as long and thick around as our shins; and feasted on tomatoes that tasted of summer, best with nothing but a sprinkling of salt. Although it wasn't all idyll. One morning I was nearly killed by a runaway hog who jumped the fence when he saw me coming his way with a pail of slop in each hand. Without thinking, I turned and ran, myopically careening (I hadn't yet brushed my teeth much less put in my contacts) in the direction of the house. Whit shouted from the porch, but slop slopping, heart hammering, three hundred pounds of pig snorting and galloping from behind, I couldn't hear him.

"Help me!" I hollered.

"Drop them!" he yelled. "Drop the pails!" Finally close enough to read his lips, I let go. Just in time. My hero, he'd saved my life. On top of which he guided that hog—Major was his name—back to his pen, and mended the fence just so. Days were like that on the farm, they started so early, with such drama, I should have been exhausted—I'm certain I was—all the more so because I couldn't sleep. Instead I lay awake through the nights, listening to the crickets and Whit's regular breathing on the other side of the wall.

But I wasn't just in love with him that July. I was in love with Roslyn, too. Roslyn—winsome and funny and deep; Roslyn, just that much older than I, a wife and mother, enchanted, enchanting; Roslyn, who kept journals in meticulous cursive, who bathed Wren in a claw-footed tub, who made soups and roasts and fat fruit pies, who listened—rolling, stuffing, patting, and kneading—nodding at me in a way that made me feel corroborated and worthy. Roslyn was Whit's friend first, but then mine, mine especially, well into the following summer and winter.

Whitney mended the hog pen before we moved back to The Spruces on top of the hill, where, all that next week, we passed each other in the corridor on our way to brush our teeth, a bit awkward for having lived together for a few days. One night I found myself in his room—just passing by, just visiting, toothbrush in hand—we two sitting on his cot, he shutting the door behind us, rolling on top of me in one deliberate move, both of us completely clothed, but the shock and the pleasure and the weight of him greater than I expected. He kissed me then, with more violence than I have ever known in a kiss, with a mouth so wide, a tongue so muscular, I wondered afterwards how he made all that room in his narrow jaw. Wondered, too, if it would happen again, and if I'd be able to slow the moment, to fix that kiss and make it perfect. I so distracted myself with wondering that I almost didn't notice that nothing between us had changed, until enough time passed that I wondered if the kiss had actually happened.

Towards the end of summer my parents came up for a weekend—to see a couple of shows, to take me to brunch—and I invited Whit to come along.

I don't remember where we went or what we ate or talked about. I only remember saying our goodbyes afterwards, all of us standing outside on the lawn, patchy in the way of worn upholstery, and dotted with dying dandelions. My mother, eyes narrowed, leaning against her Ford

Country Squire, with her arms folded across her chest, followed Whitney's progress back to the house, up the decrepit front steps, onto the sagging porch and in the front door, shutting the screen behind him. "He's not for you, Dinah," she said, and before I could respond, "Trust me, dear, he isn't for you."

I took it as a put-down: I wasn't good enough for Whitney, in spite of a hope chest of sorts and my own very fine sterling service for twelve. I was a peasant, built solid and sturdy—a Jew—dark of feature, loud, not refined enough, not in his league. But I wasn't listening, was I? She hadn't said I wasn't for *him*. She said *he* wasn't for me. Deflated, I caved in on myself, went quiet with anger and hurt. I'd prove her wrong. I'd prove her wrong over and over again: I'd chase the wrong guys, get involved in the wrong relationships. I could have whoever I wanted, I was right for absolutely everybody. All that time wasted. If I'd only been listening—some people weren't right for *me*.

Years later, Emma the Redhead married a doctor or lawyer and moved back to Atlanta or Richmond or Nashville. Whit moved to one end of Manhattan to try his fortune, and I to the other to try mine. Roslyn and Geoff eventually divorced, so I heard. She married someone else and had another child, long after we stopped talking to each other, long after she wrote to say I wasn't somebody she wanted to know.

A few days before, she'd been in touch to make plans for a visit, a weekend in the city. I sat by the phone Friday and Saturday nights, finally leaving an outgoing message on my answering machine when I left to buy the paper on Sunday morning: "Roslyn, if that's you . . ." Late that night, fingers trembling, I tried her at home in New Hampshire from my rotary phone, half-expecting no answer, or news of some disaster, indignant when she picked up the line as if nothing had happened, as if I hadn't been waiting to hear from her for three days running. She didn't have the time, she said, to talk. Towards the end of the following week, her letter arrived in my box in the foyer.

"Just tell me," I asked my mother. "What did I do?"

"Never mind," she answered. "That's it, let it go. You'll never hear from her again."

✍

Not so long ago I saw Roslyn's name on the roster at a conference where I was also presenting a paper. After her talk, I waited in line for her. She was rounder and grayer than the woman I remembered; I'd never have known her if I hadn't been determined to find her in that hall. When she caught my gaze, she started and recovered—not from surprise, but with the shock of recognition, my name on her lips. She reached over the person in front of me to take my hand.

"Dinah, can you forgive me for being such an asshole thirty years ago?"

Without considering—wanting only to be magnanimous, and in that way to tease out not just remorse but genuine regret—I answered that I could. I asked about Wren. I think she said she was a grandmother. She mentioned her second husband, and her son, and I waxed effusive. We spoke only of her and hers, as though only she had lived the three decades between, as if I were still the besotted young woman at her kitchen counter. Both of us on our way to other events, we agreed we'd be in touch. We didn't bump into each other again that week, nor did either of us make contact afterwards.

✍

Whitney—my old, good friend—stopped acting long ago, went to work for a furniture maker, and lives alone in Vermont. He skis all winter, gardens all summer, puts up preserves, bakes his own bread, sings in a local choir, and sends his godchild, my son, birthday and Christmas cards every year. He's afraid of what he wants, which is to find a partner, a man with whom he can make a real life. My mother was right: he wasn't for me. But somewhere inside him is the boy who kissed me with a mouth like a cave. Somewhere inside me is the girl who didn't sleep for a week for wanting him. Somewhere in Roslyn is, if not curiosity about the woman I've become, remembered affection, I hope, for that misguided girl. In me, even now, the inspiration of her competence and steady gaze. Somewhere in her daughter, Wren, who must be thirtysomething, is the towhead captured in primary colors, her father's artwork evidence of a life she may not remember. For me, the image of that toddler a spark, the first glimmer of the idea of a daughter of my own, whose baby photo, creased and faded, I keep in my wallet. In her, then, my almost-grown daughter, is a baby girl in red overalls with yellow hair. And inside her grandmother, my mother, is the woman who used to know things having to do with me before I knew them myself.

As for Geoff, the artist whose half dozen pieces I have on my walls—he's as featureless in my memory as the people in his posters, as if the specifics were beside the point. So it is with this picture inside the picture. True to Geoff's signature style, it's blank, so that we cannot see what it is the man with the cigarette ponders. Surely, it's not my life on display, stirred up from the deep, rippling across the surface of the frame inside the frame. No. In my mind, it's a picture of a man looking at a picture of a man looking at a picture. Things disappearing into things disappearing into things.

LETTER TO DAD

IF I FINISHED it (and how could I ever finish it?) what would I do with it—what then? Put it in a bottle and toss it into the ocean? Tie it to one end of a helium balloon? Take a match to it and watch it curl into ash? This is assuming I print it out—choose a font, set the margins, find the right stationery; a creamy cardstock, or no—something lighter, something tissue paper thin (those old blue aerograms), something with wings, that might take the air of its own accord. Something green, naturally—organic, compostable—since who says you reside in the atmosphere as opposed to the earth?

As if there were a way to reach you, Dad. As if you exist.

Dear Dad,

The kids—they're so big—I'm wanting to show them off, to watch you watching them. Though the truth is (would I say so if you were alive? Or would I try to flatter you?), Jake looks less like you than he did. And (would I tell you this?) I see my mother in his face, too—in those high bones and that finely sculpted nose. And everyone else sees

Fred. "You look just like your dad," people tell Jake. But when he and I meet in the upstairs bath, when we stand before the mirror, one of us washing his or her hands, the other peering into the glass, when we catch each other's eye and grin, we are complicit, a conspiracy of two: "You look just like your dad," I say. "Yeah, right," says he. And we laugh. If I'm objective? He looks something like Fred, yes. And something like me. And I look like you. Do other people do this? Do other people compare pictures of themselves to pictures of their parents, not for the resemblance per se, but to find out how they're faring? Aging better or worse? Do we ever see ourselves as we are? These crow's feet, Dad—just exactly like yours.

But what would you look like now? Fifteen years since you were killed. Fifteen years since a couple of teenagers decided—so stupid, so cavalier—to rob and abduct you: and that wasn't enough, they stabbed and stoned you, too, then left you to die on the New York side of the Hudson. On a clear September day. Fifteen years later, I still don't know how long it took you to die; if you knew you were dying; if the sun was in your eyes. But this is exposition, isn't it, for the sake of the reader— and smells false in that way; though that last part, Dad, I really do wonder. I really do still want to know. However. I don't need to tell you what happened—not in a letter meant only for you. Unless—would you need exposition, Dad? Or would you remember? And if you remembered, would you be angry? Do the dead remember to be angry? For the record: I don't remember you angry, not often, not much. Indifferent, yes. Occasionally disgusted. But angry? With me? Seldom.

Dear Dad,

Bear with me: I know you don't especially want to talk about books. But I read this novel: the inner lives of three women revealed, and all of them circling a portrait—the image of a dead man—who was this one's lover and that one's husband, and, having to do with his importance to this one and that one, becomes the third one's fantasy: the dead as glamorous, mysterious, ageless—eternally wise and withholding (not to mention attractive)—each woman cultivating a relationship with the dead guy as if he gave a shit. (My words, not the author's, though she put the idea in my head.) Such a misguided relationship we have with the dead, right? As if they—you—were thinking of us. Which they're not—you're not—he isn't in the story, the dead guy, I mean, he's long dead, after all. Therefore not following the women's progress; therefore, not aware of himself as pivotal in their lives—not inclined to choose one of the three as his favorite. And why should he get to be so important anyway, dead as he is. Right?

As if I'm asking you. As if you have an opinion. Yes, yes, I know: were you alive, you'd want me to defer to you as if you did, of course you would. But you don't. And you wouldn't have if you were alive. First, you wouldn't have read this novel. Too old-fashioned for the likes of you. But who am I to weigh in on your reading habits, Dad. Not that you care, having nothing to do with your literary tastes. You don't mind because you're dead. You're dead, Dad.

Thornton Wilder got close to the truth of this, I think, though I'm miffed with him, too (see, it's the living who get pissy, isn't it, the living who endow not just each other but the dead, too, with feelings and qualities they couldn't possibly have); miffed, now that I consider, for his having pretended not to be sentimental, and nonetheless coming up with this notion that the dead are collectively and deliberately indifferent to the living; as if the dead were capable of being deliberate much less indifferent. Did you ever see Our Town? *When you were in high school maybe, or in college? I saw a production not long ago, sparsely conceived in a gymnasium of a theater, under house lights, no props, no costumes—not in the first and second acts anyway—flatly delivered by actors in ordinary dress: just life as usual (the way we actually live it), until after Emily's funeral in the third, when Emily, left behind in the cemetery, wants to remember what it was like to be alive. Pick an ordinary day, caution the dead (who know what she's in for), and she picks her twelfth birthday; the memory evoked on a proscenium; dramatized, with lights and scenery, and real bacon frying in a pan: to prove what? Not only that we don't appreciate what we have when we have it—that was Wilder's point—but that we can't. If we could, if we did—if, in the* moment, we were shading, coloring, rueing, and remembering—we wouldn't be living. Meanwhile, the past rushing in, the smell and the taste of it—almost unbearable. The ordinary reimagined, too vivid, too painful—which is why in Our Town, the dead choose indifference. They choose it—that's the implication. Oh Dad, if you were only indifferent to me; if it were only that. I could almost live with that, since it would imply, wouldn't it, that I'll also get to go on somewhere somehow, however indifferent I might decide to be. But it isn't true, is it? I'll be dead, too, one of these days. Just like you.

That being so, I have some things to tell you before I lose my nerve, start to feel ridiculous, or fall off the curb and get hit by a truck. As if you were listening. Although I do feel that you'd listen better now than you did then—you, chewing that cuticle, staring off into space, fiddling with the remote in search of a score or a headline. Or am I wrong about that? What were you thinking, Dad? Were you as bored as I thought you were—at the circus, at the play, on the slopes, by the pool, in the car—with only me for company? And even then, I the sort of person— the sort of little girl—who couldn't suffer silence; silence frightened me. Silence might pry me from my place on the planet and send me spinning out unmoored, untethered to anyone or anything. So: Were you disinterested, Dad? Or were you listening the whole time?

Dear Dad,

I'm over fifty. No need to make an announcement, you might say— but I thought you should know.

Eliza graduated from college with honors last May.

Jake is a sophomore at the same school in Boston and beginning to embrace the other coast for the other planet it is.

They're funny and beautiful, Dad.

And they remember you—not well—but we had all those videotapes converted to DVDs. And there are photos of you all over the house. And yesterday, for instance, I noticed one of your old sweaters in the laundry basket, having just come out of the washer. I was about to hang it over the shower in the upstairs bath, but Eliza, who'd brought it home *from college (it belongs to her now) told me she puts it in the dryer all the time.*

So you know? I don't speak to your son.

Nor do I talk to your wife but once a year, to wish her happy birthday and to thank her for sending those paltry Christmas checks. (Well, they are. They're paltry.)

Would you be interested to know? My mother is well. She and I have weathered much conflict, and—you might even be gratified to hear—much of it caused by the way you died, by the way I was compelled to mourn, to show my loyalty; misplaced in her view, necessary in mine. "Pay attention to the living," she said. And "I'm sorry for you, Dinah, but I didn't kill your father." And finally, "He wasn't a hero, you know." Of course not. Heroes are few and far between. I wasn't inclined to make a saint of you, Dad. Nor did my grief indicate for even a moment that I am not, first and always, Leah's daughter—that she doesn't continue to be my most profound and sustained influence.

Speaking of heroic, Ron is eighty-five. Seemingly impervious to the passing of time till last year, when a malignant tumor on his hip cost him his pelvis, which was removed and replaced with a younger one (from a cadaver), a nearly perfect fit. But the operation necessitated severing and reattaching nerves, ligaments, arteries, which means he's not as active as he was, though neither is he about to give up or give in, not my dad. See that? I forget myself: and I wonder, I can't help wondering—all of us so careful all the time, that is each of you, you and Ron, determined not to mention the other dad, as if he didn't exist. Were you grateful to him? Did you know how lucky I was and am that he was willing and generous? That he let himself love me? That he loves my children? Moreover, they're unburdened with the confusion I felt growing up; not unaware, not unsympathetic, but they rightly see my doubt and dilemma—who was I? where did I belong? how not to offend? how to prove myself worthy?—as my problem, not theirs. Not that Ron, or anyone else, meant for me to worry or doubt, of course not. And he maybe wouldn't understand (wouldn't even believe) that I can't help wishing that my children knew you: my father. What difference would it make to Eliza and Jake, beloved as they are? None, perhaps. None at all. But it would have been good for you, Dad, that's sure. To claim them every once in a while, to bask in their uncomplicated affection as, I'm thankful to say, Ron—Dad—does without question.

Anyway. He was older than you, remember? By now he's outlived you by a couple of decades—even my mother is ten years older than you were when you died. And I—I am only ten years younger. Ten years younger than my own father.

Dear Dad,

A friend asks when she will recover from the death of her dad. Never, I say, you will never recover, you're not supposed to recover, what sort of people would we be if we did? What would that say about us as a species? I once heard a writer remark, No recovery, only integration. You—alive and dead—I've absorbed your trajectory as part of my own: How would you feel about that? What would you say? See, this is what we do to the dead. We ask inappropriate questions. We make inappropriate demands. We want your approval. We impose and insist. Assume and presume. Much as we do with the living, I suppose, but the living live to contradict us and set us straight. The dead—the dead, unchecked, just get bigger and bigger in our imaginations; we blow them up into beach ball versions of themselves—versions of ourselves.

Dear Dad,

You'd have me mourn you, wouldn't you? You'd have me remember. And regret. And want more.

I want people to mourn me. Whether or not I'm available to enjoy it. For their sakes, let them miss me; let me have been a person worth missing. Except that person? She wouldn't be wasting time wanting others to suffer her death; she'd be more generous than that, and more present, and less self-involved; she wouldn't suppose there are answers in the afterlife—wouldn't ingratiate herself to anybody, living or dead— she'd only live as well as she could, not as if she might die some day,

*and what then? Only as if she will certainly die some day, and in the
meantime there are things to do . . .*

Dear Dad,

*I'd never have written you this letter if you were alive. Not because
there weren't things unsaid between us, but because, no excuses, you
wouldn't have been a good pen pal. But now—beyond reproach as you
are—I can go on as I please without feeling I've gone too far or said too
much.*

*Dad, do you ever see Gramma and Grampa? Do you bump into each
other's molecules and atoms? And, if you do, are you appropriately
electrified? Do you bounce away then or glom on (for dear life) without
knowing? Dad—do you feel about dead people as I do?*

*My friends, some of them see ghosts—hear them and feel them—I'm
the one who knows better? Of course I don't.*

Dear Dad—

*You would have thought I was all grown up when you were mur-
dered: a woman in her forty-first year, a woman with children, a
husband, a house, cars, dogs—a woman well-acquainted with failure.
If this hadn't happened to you, what would have happened to me? And
is this what we do? Do we let our lives just happen? Do we afterwards
claim to have had any say?*

*And, Dad, do you belong in this object parade, from which you've
been conspicuously missing till now? Why haven't I been able to bring
you to life from the silver cigarette case that came in a box after you
died; or those heavy, gold monogrammed cufflinks; or the tie pin,
cheap, but engraved with your initials, that I wore every day for a year;
or from one of the shirts that hang in the back of my closet?*

And even so, Dad? I've been holding your place in line.

INSTRUCTIONS

IF I WERE brave, if I could commit to anything, I'd say scatter me in Elysian Park.

You don't want me to take you to Nantucket? Fred asks. And this is absurd. This is the sort of thing that puts me in a fury: as if I have any connection to Nantucket—as if he does. That's not just the road not taken. Nantucket, for chrissakes. It wasn't ever in the offing, not for a minute.

Nantucket, I say. (I spit, actually. Because I'm rude sometimes. And unkind.) *Nantucket, why?*

Because we spent New Year's Eve on that island three decades ago? Because, show off that I was, I stripped down under frigid skies and ran into the ocean that last gray day of December? Because my toes froze on the bike ride back to the inn, where he bought me a toddy in the bar, then took my feet into his lap and massaged them back to life. Because, that night, in the restaurant, bathed, fragrant, swathed in velvet—a deep rose-hued dress with a sweetheart neckline—I went him one better: lifted the long starched cloth that draped our corner table (this, between the oysters and the entrees) and went down on my knees under there, as if for a lost fork. Because, though we couldn't have known, we were starting our lives together, that's the reason, according to him (such a romantic); implicit, of course, that I would therefore choose to spend the rest of my life on Nantucket. Or—not my life—my what? As if eternity as well as the other coast, belongs to me.

Puts a spot on the absurdity of choosing a location—unless I do it for his pleasure and convenience, which brings me right back where I started: were I able to summon the courage of my convictions, to actually entertain the idea of my demise, I'd shrug off the whole idea of exotic locales. I'd insist, or at least surrender to spending the rest of time—not my days, exactly, but time itself—in the park not a quarter mile east, where we've walked our dogs for twenty-five years, assuming, that is, that he stays in this house, on this street, in this town. And absurdity aside—to believe I can or should dictate his choice (he will put me where he pleases)—what about the pretention? As if to impress, whom, each other? As if to fulfill some fantasy scenario—too much, too late? As if I'd have the nerve to tell him to trek, for my sake, to Paris, London, or Rome; to the mountains of New Hampshire; to the Cape (the bay side, if you please); to Manhattan. Although—Manhattan—isn't that where I belong? *Bosh. Tell the truth, why don't you? As if you ever once came up out of a subway and knew where you were.* And yet: for the longest time, I kept one of those pins in the bottom of my pencil jar, the size of a silver dollar, white with red letters: *Broadway, I'll be back,* it read. As if, all over again. What did I think? That the kids would grow up and I wouldn't? That we'd return to New York and be whom? Ourselves? But we, ourselves, happen to live just over the rise from Dodger Stadium on the other side of Elysian Park. *Elysian!*—we, who don't believe in that shit (perhaps *because* we don't believe in that shit) aren't paying attention, are we? But c'mon now, we're looking to rest in a *better* place?

No better place. Still, I'm one to keep my options open: as if, when I've been reduced to ash, when the dregs of me are rattling around in the bottom of a canister, I'll have options . . .

I'll tell you what, love. You go first. I'll shuttle you wherever you please, though how to abandon you there (don't you want me to visit you?), when the only heaven we'll ever know is here? Meanwhile, you and I foolishly yakking, planning, squinting into the smog *as if* there were something above and beyond.

EPILOGUE

WHAT IF I'D chosen other things—?

I could as easily have picked my grandmother's tennis bracelet, which I wear with the little black dress. Or the potted hibiscus out there on the deck, a substitute for the one that I moved from the East Side to the West and back again when I lived in Manhattan. Or the circle of sea glass, heavy and green, the lip of a bottle Fred found on Kingsbury beach in Wellfleet and passed on to me for my collection over there on the floor, in a big glass jar. So many jars, come to think of it—such a variety of containers: a tin bowl big enough to bathe a baby in (and we did); a basket I found on a side street in Hollywood, sturdy enough to hold logs by the hearth; a ceramic wine pitcher, a gift from our waiter in a tiny restaurant on the edge of the Campo de'Fiori in Rome. The late '80s, it was, and us just married—I'd been cast on a television show that shot all over Europe, and people, friends and strangers, kept giving us things. We gave each other things, too. Fred bought me a slim painted box in a Budapest, and, in Malta, I found him a pair of lions, lacquered squares with heads and manes, big enough to hold stamps or paperclips, meant to suggest the original cats, the ones outside the library on Fifth Avenue, where we each of us worked for a friend whose wedding present to us was a framed poster: *A Building to Celebrate,* it reads, in honor of the Forty-Second Street branch, which turned seventy-five the year we were married—and it hangs in our living room over the upside-down breakfront.

Presents—there's a category unto itself. For instance: Ron's brown fedora ("Do you like it? Take it then"), or the beaded bag, given to me by Ella, his mother—for whom we pretend Eliza wasn't named, because Jews don't name babies for the living. (Except, when a person is beloved and nearing ninety-three—then some of us do.) The Eames chair in my office—from Leah, of course—purchased before I was born and a bit worse for wear, but one of these days, as with Charlie's piano, we'll have it restored and refinished just so. Any number of books and records and utensils, slightly obscure: the sterling silver dieter's fork, four-pronged, but one of them curls up and around and so limits intake; two Bakelite napkin rings (a red duck, a green bunny); the shapely brass corkscrew, not a present, not really, though nobody seems to mind that I pilfered it from 1019 decades ago. Say, if I weren't about finished—I might explain how in a frenzy I ransacked drawers, cupboards, and shelves for Eliza, who just a few months ago packed up her car and drove to New York, where she's living in a brownstone on the Upper West side, with (among other things), a yellow colander missing its handles, a scarred old kettle, a stack of cloth napkins, three loaf pans, a muffin tin, a red sugar bowl, a pair of candlesticks, and some buffalo china. Which brings me to *China* (see how one thing leads to another?): it's framed—the place, I mean—on the wall in our bedroom. And that's worth mentioning: how Fred took a scissors to a continent—cut China from his father's old atlas and gave it to me for our vicennial, our twentieth—because, tradition notwithstanding, we didn't need actual china: because, said he, he'd have taken me to China if he could. And I was as delighted with China-in-a-frame as if he had. Funny to consider: were I to write about the old atlas, I'd might find myself yearning for places I've only dreamed of going. Whereas to write about the missing page, the framed map on the wall in our bedroom, is to yearn for the road we've actually traveled, which, but for the evidence—China, framed on the wall (among other objects)—might also be a dream. This is how it works, isn't it? We attach meaning to things, and things to meaning: endow them one way or another as if to prove to ourselves that we are who we are; this life really happened; we really have traveled this far in time and space.

Take the seals. How have I left them out? Three sizes, made of pewter—they belonged to Fred's mother. They sit on his desk. They comfort and signify—but not just for him. I love them, too, for their shape and heft and featureless mystery. And because they remind me: we were on our honeymoon. We'd only just arrived in Big Sur, weren't even unpacked when we decided to take a drive along the coast, and not far from our hotel we pulled into a rest stop for a better view. Next to us there, leaning against an ugly Winnebago, a middle-aged woman, one hand on her hip, smoked and fumed, while her husband, just paces away, peered over the guardrail and down the cliffs.

We got out of the car.

The woman jutted her chin in the man's direction and made a face. "He thinks he heard a seal," she said.

The man looked back and noticed us then. "Come look," he shouted. "There's a seal down here, I heard a seal!"

"We've been standing around for a half an hour," said his wife. "Nothing down there, not a damn thing." She took a long drag.

Politely, we nodded—sheepishly sidestepped over to her husband to have a look for ourselves. He was wearing a baseball cap, I remember, and wire-rimmed glasses and his shirt, buttoned high, strained across his belly.

"It's down there somewhere," he said. "I know it is."

His wife stubbed out her cigarette with one shoe. "Let's get going," she bellowed. "Come on, already, I'm hungry," she said. "Let's get on the road."

The man frowned at the surf below. "I'm sure I heard a seal," he said. "You keep looking," he told us, sotto voce. "I bet you'll see it." He walked back to his wife then, and they both climbed into the cab.

And we looked down. The cliffs were vertical and jagged, the water gray-green, violent and foamy. And so many stones, glistening and smooth, big black stones along the narrow strip of sand at the water's edge, and on top of slabs of rock, too, stones, huge and wet and glinting in the sun. Just as the Winnebago pulled away from us and onto the highway, they started to move. And bark. And float. Hundreds more emerged then, more stones swimming out from underneath a ledge, they slipped and splashed into the water, a flock, a pod—a sign, it seemed to us, a sign in the parade of signs—a chorus of well-wishers, a harem of seals.

Now this here, this *is* a dream: We forgot to get married and we never had children—we never got around to any of it. And now, in the dream, he's had it with me, he's leaving, he says. In the dream, I'm thirty, thirty-five, forty, forty-five, fifty . . . That is, I'm as old as I am. The dream is recurring, but different from the others, the ones in which I'm lost in the dark, barefoot and trudging uphill or wading through water with all my belongings balanced on my head like a picture in *National Geographic*. This dream, unlike those, is so *real*, which is maybe why I'm not able to wake myself up. In this dream, he's my very last chance at a real life—he is my real life—and he's walking away. In this dream—though I've shrugged him off a half a dozen times during the day—though I've been snippy and critical and rude (maybe *because* I've been all those things), though I've thought more than once I'd just as soon live by myself (that way the counters would stay clean and I could be as selfish as I am), it's Fred who decides he can't take anymore. In the dream, as in life, he is even and rational and kind. *It just isn't worth it*, he tells me. He's not changing his mind. *But, but,* I wail, *we forgot to get married. Can't we get married? Can't we have a couple of kids? Weren't we supposed to have a couple of kids, please?* In real life, he saves me then. "Don't cry," he says, touching my shoulder. "Dinah, wake up," he says. And I do.

One evening not long after Jake had followed Eliza to the east coast for college, we were driving through Hollywood when we saw this little family—a couple with two babies— standing on a corner near Melrose and La Brea, waiting for the light to change.

It was dusk on a Sunday in autumn, the color fast draining from the sky, the storefronts dark and closed, the streets fairly empty. We were on our way back to Echo Park from an event on the west side where we hadn't even tried to have a happy time. We'd imagined that it would be good for us, wallowing as we were in misplaced and embarrassing sorrow, to get out into the day. Hadn't we known the kids would leave? Wasn't that the idea, after all? Of course it was. Even so we couldn't accept, not then, not yet, that the house had always been generously sized for just us two. We couldn't know we'd eventually revel not only in Eliza and Jake's independence, but in our own, rediscovered and re-stored. But if we were a few inches shy of remembering that we'd cho-sen each other in the first place—that was the point and the reason—we were also utterly in sync, we two: united, from the moment we arrived on the other side of town, in our desire to go home and continue to feel sorry for ourselves. The party—our party—appeared to be over, or hap-pening elsewhere without us anyway. A tenuous connection, I know (hyperbolic, to boot) but we both, Fred and I, felt all hollowed out that day. Like defunct pinatas, cracked beyond repair, as if constructed from papier mache.

But then there they were, a family of four.

"Look," I said, pointing with my chin (the best I could manage) as we cruised to a stop. It was windy: the woman's hair blew across her mouth, and she let it, both arms wrapped around the bundle on her chest—yel-low? pale blue?—one hand cradling the infant's tiny hooded head. On the other side of the empty stroller between them, the man held the hand of a toddler, fair like his mother, bouncing up and down. We watched, both of us mesmerized, as the light went green—no traffic behind us, no need to drive on.

"They have no idea what they're in for," I said.

"No, they don't," said Fred. "But they'll figure it out."

And they crossed then, in crooked single file, the man scooping up the boy and waiting for her to go first with the baby, then following behind.

ACKNOWLEDGMENTS

Thanks to the editors of the following journals and anthologies, in which versions of some of these essays were first published:

Get on the Bus
Superstition Review
The Coachella Review
The Los Angeles Times
Becoming
The Kenyon Review Online
Creative Nonfiction
Chaparral
Defunct
The Mom Egg
Prime Number Magazine
AGNI
Water~Stone
Brevity

Spaces
The Southampton Review
The California Prose Directory
The Harvard Review

Also, I'm tipping my hat to Denise Benjamin and Dolores Patton, of Yellow Cluster at the Open Charter School, who produced and directed the original event.

And to the kitchen table regulars—Ellen Collett, Lisa Alexander, Laura Simko, Hillary Evans, and Jeff Duncan—who listened to some very early drafts.

And to Sariah Dorbin, Alice Mattison, Brighde Mullins, Erika Schickel, Leslie Schwartz, and David Ulin, for good cheer and good counsel.

And to David Biespiel, Sven Birkerts, Bernard Cooper, Amy Gerstler, Judith Kitchen, and Susan Scarf Merrell, all of whom went above and beyond.

I'm grateful to everyone at Counterpoint, Dan Smetanka, especially, for his mind-boggling intuition, generosity, clarity, and perspective.

And to Ron and Leah Lenney—my parents—for all they have given.

As for my loves, Fred, Eliza, and Jake: without you, nothing (no thing) would be the same.

Dinah Lenney
November, 2013.

Printed in the United States
by Baker & Taylor Publisher Services